QUICK, CHEAP

COMFORT FOOD

100+ Fresh Recipes for
Meals in a Hurry

VICTORIA SHEARER

SELLER
PUBLISHING

D0006549

Dedication

Hey, Junior Julia. It's me, Mini Martha. You were my inspiration!

Published by Sellers Publishing, Inc.

Text copyright © 2009 Victoria Shearer
All rights reserved.

Edited by Megan Hiller
Sellers Publishing, Inc.

161 John Roberts Road, South Portland, Maine 04106
For ordering information:
(800) 625-3386 toll free
Visit our Web site: www.sellerspublishing.com • E-mail: rsp@rsvp.com

ISBN: 13: 978-1-4162-0781-8

Library of Congress Control Number: 2009923846

10 9 8 7 6 5 4 3 2

Printed and bound in China.

CONTENTS

R ich, unpretentious, feel-good food. That's comfort food. Whether it's a taste memory from your childhood — spaghetti and meatballs, mac 'n' cheese, peanut butter and jelly — or a guilty adult pleasure — chocolate cake, a half-pound burger, a loaded baked potato — comfort food is personal.

Maybe you're tired, you've had a bad day, or the world just doesn't seem like a very nice place at the moment. You might long for a taste of the peaceful times you remember growing up. You want to feed your family good, healthy, comforting foods, but you don't have a lot of time . . . or money.

Quick, Cheap Comfort Food shows you the way, with more than 100 easy-to-make, inexpensive, comforting recipes. Cheaper and more nutritious than take-out or fast food, most dishes can be prepared in fewer than 30 minutes and all cost less than $4 per serving.

Some days you may wish you could just take something out of the freezer in the morning that you can pop in the oven after work or after a long day of kids and carpooling. In *Quick, Cheap Comfort Food*, you'll also find recipes that you can make ahead, in fewer than 30 minutes, when you have some weekend time to putter in the kitchen. Simply freeze the dishes until you need them. The defrosted dishes will cook up in minutes, while you relax and put your feet up.

And because sometimes you simply want to come home at day's end to the intoxicating odors of something cooking in the kitchen, you'll find some slow-cooker meals. Load up the slow cooker in the morning and your meal cooks itself while you go about your life. It's ready when you are.

A well-stocked pantry and freezer are every cook's best friends, and at mealtime can make the difference between stress and solace. A complete inventory list at the conclusion of *Quick, Cheap Comfort Food* is all you'll need to make every recipe in this book without having to make a special trip to the store. And armed with an arsenal of time- and money-saving tips, you'll be able to share a world of nourishing food in a nurturing environment with those you love.

How To Use This Book

The scout motto: "Be prepared" applies to cooking as well as to life in general. Before you begin making any of the recipes in this book, take a couple of minutes to assemble all the necessary ingredients, measuring utensils, mixing bowls, cooking equipment, etc. You will be amazed at how much time and how many steps this simple routine will save you.

You'll find the recipes herein sprinkled with graphic icons, designed to provide you with useful information at a glance. You'll quickly see if a recipe can be made ahead ▦ or prepared in a slow cooker ◉.

We've figured the approximate cost per serving for each recipe so you can plan your weekly budget.

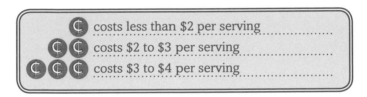

For each recipe, we have included actual prep time ◉ (hands-on time) and cooking time ◉ (hands-off time) to assist you in your meal planning.

Finally, a potpourri of useful tips ◉ includes suggestions for substitutions and innovations within each recipe, helping you cut time and costs even more.

Look for the detailed pantry, refrigerator, and freezer list in the back of the book. This comprehensive survey lists every ingredient you'll need to prepare any recipe in this book, as well as necessary kitchen equipment and supplies. You'll find more time- and money-saving tips here as well.

What's for Breakfast . . . Lunch . . . Dinner. . . Dessert ?????

This book — *Quick, Cheap Comfort Food* — is divided into nine chapters. Most of the recipes in "Breakfast All Day" are hearty enough to double as a quick weekday dinner. "Out of Hand" shines the spotlight on some great, speedy meals on the run, including sandwiches, burgers, brats, and pizza.

Super comforting on a cold winter day, "Some Like It In The Pot" focuses on soups, stew, chili, and chowder. "Oodles of Noodles" provides myriad pasta recipes, including some make-ahead and slow-cooker dishes.

When you want to serve something special to family or friends but you don't have a lot of extra time or money to spend on the task, "When Company Comes" provides applause-winning solutions. And if you want to put all the necessary food groups together tastefully in one dish, look no further than "One-Dish Dinners."

"Farmers' Market" highlights salads and vegetable dishes, while "Side Shows" rounds out the meal with potatoes, rice, beans, and breads.

And, of course, what is more comforting than dessert? "Sweet Eats" has something to satisfy every sweet tooth.

When asked what she considers comfort food, a friend stated: "It depends on what needs comforting." *Quick, Cheap Comfort Food* has all the bases covered. Comfort yourself. Start cooking!

Breakfast All Day

• Hearty Fare for Any Meal •

Sunflower Eggs Benedict

Skillet Scramble

Spinach, Mushroom, Cheddar Omelet

Busy Morning Breakfast Cupcakes

Southwestern Scrambled EggBeaters Rollup

Ham-Artichoke-Tomato Frittata

Potato Pancakes

Apple-Sausage Puffed Pancake

Bacon–Four-Cheese Waffles

Stuffed Orange French Toast

Loaded Oatmeal Mix

Sunflower Eggs Benedict

You'll find no scheming traitor with this Benedict, but you will trade time-consuming egg poaching and tedious whisking over a double boiler for a fast, easy rendition of the all-time favorite. The presentation rivals Brennan's of New Orleans.

1 (5-ounce) package round Canadian bacon (8 slices)

4 large eggs

1 tablespoon fresh snipped parsley or 1 teaspoon dried

1 tablespoon fresh snipped dill or 1 teaspoon dried

Salt and freshly ground black pepper

4 tablespoons (½ stick) butter

1 cup water

1 (1.25-ounce) package McCormick Hollandaise Sauce Mix

2 English muffins

Preheat oven to 350°F. Coat each of 4 round ramekins with vegetable cooking spray. Place I bacon round snugly in the bottom of each ramekin. Cut 4 bacon rounds into quarters, making half-moon triangles. Place 4 bacon quarters in each ramekin (point side up, flat side down), forming "petals" around the inner side of each cup. Break I egg in the center of the petals in each cup. Season each egg with a sprinkling of parsley and dill, and salt and freshly ground black pepper to taste. Place ramekins on a baking sheet and bake for 15 minutes, until whites are just set and yolks are still runny.

While eggs are baking, melt butter in a small saucepan over medium-low heat. Add water and sauce mix and whisk to combine. Raise heat to medium and cook, stirring frequently, until sauce begins to boil, about I minute. Reduce heat to low and cook until thickened, whisking frequently, about I minute. (If sauce has thickened before eggs are done, remove pan from heat and reheat, whisking constantly, just before serving.)

Cut each English muffin in half and toast.

To assemble: Place I muffin half on each of 4 plates. Run a kitchen knife around the edges of each egg cup. Using a salad fork, gently lift each egg "flower" out of cup and place atop English muffin. Spoon hollandaise sauce over each serving.

You'll need four ¼-cup round ramekins or custard cups for this recipe. To serve a large group of guests, simply use a ¼-cup muffin tin instead of the ramekins. Be sure to fill any unused muffin cups with water to ensure even cooking.

Serves: 4 | 10 minutes | 15–20 minutes

Skillet Scramble

This tasty, healthy, efficient way to clean out your refrigerator allows you to rival the best restaurant breakfast chef. Grab the eggs; pull out whatever suits your fancy from the vegetable, meat, and cheese drawers; and scramble away.

4 large eggs

Dash of Tabasco or hot sauce

2 tablespoons olive oil

¼ cup finely diced green or red bell peppers

¼ cup sliced mushrooms

¼ cup seeded, finely diced tomatoes

2 tablespoons finely sliced scallions or snipped chives

¼ cup finely diced ham, or crumbled crisp bacon, or crumbled cooked sausage

¼ cup finely snipped baby spinach, stems removed

⅓ cup grated cheddar, Swiss, or Monterey Jack cheese

Salt and freshly ground black pepper

With a wire whisk, beat eggs and hot sauce together in a medium bowl. Set aside.

Heat oil in a large nonstick skillet over medium-low heat. Add peppers and mushrooms. Sauté, stirring occasionally, until vegetables are soft and the liquid from the mushrooms has evaporated, about 2 minutes. Add tomatoes, scallions or chives, and meats. Sauté for 2 minutes, stirring frequently. Add spinach, stir, and cook for 1 minute more.

Pour beaten eggs over skillet ingredients and cook over medium-low heat. (Cook eggs slowly so that chopped vegetables and meats are spread throughout the eggs.) Turn eggs frequently with a firm spatula until eggs are soft but cooked through.

Remove skillet from heat and stir in cheese. Serve scramble from hot skillet. Season with salt and freshly ground black pepper to taste.

 Follow the proportions in this recipe, but change the ingredients any way you'd like. Use a combo of cheeses or meats, change herbs, use whatever fresh vegetables you have on hand. Be sure to first sauté those veggies needing more cooking time.

Prep all your ingredients before you start cooking. Cut mushroom slices in half so that their size is comparable to the diced veggies. To prepare spinach, stack leaves and roll them like a cigar. Cut thin strips with kitchen scissors.

Serves: 2–3 | 15–20 minutes | 🕐 10–15 minutes

Spinach, Mushroom, Cheddar Omelet

Two dates are printed on egg cartons: One is the Sell By date; the other is a 9-digit number called the Julian date, the last three numbers of which indicates the day of the year the eggs were packed. For instance: 087 would be March 28 (the 87th day of the year). The Sell By date should be no more than 30 days after the Julian date and preferably as close to Julian date as possible for the eggs to be fresh.

2 tablespoons butter, divided
⅓ cup chopped sweet onions, like Vidalia
4 ounces fresh mushrooms, sliced
3 large handfuls fresh baby spinach, washed and dried
¼ teaspoon salt
¼ teaspoon black pepper
5 extra-large eggs, beaten
½ cup shredded sharp cheddar cheese

Melt 1 tablespoon butter in a medium nonstick skillet over medium heat. Add onions and mushrooms and sauté for about 2 minutes, stirring occasionally, until they have softened. Remove from heat and set onions and mushrooms aside.

Meanwhile, in a separate medium, dry skillet over medium heat, sauté spinach until wilted, stirring constantly, about 1 minute. Remove to a small plate.

Melt remaining 1 tablespoon butter in still-warm skillet over medium heat. Combine salt and pepper with beaten eggs, then add eggs, swirling to coat pan. When eggs just begin to set around the edges, pull edges back with a small spatula and tip skillet so that liquid egg mixture fills in the edge gaps. Continue pulling and tipping until all but a thin film of egg has set.

Reduce heat to low. Sprinkle egg mixture with onions, mushrooms, spinach, and cheese. Using a large, firm spatula, fold one-half of the egg mixture over the other half. Cut omelet in half and serve immediately.

 You can substitute most any of your favorite vegetables, breakfast meats, or cheeses for those in this recipe. The important thing to do when making this French-style omelet is to constantly pull cooked eggs slightly toward the center while tipping the liquid eggs to the outer rim. The result is a light, airy egg envelope, encasing a myriad of tasty ingredients. The omelet is great for breakfast, lunch, or a light supper.

Serves: 2 | 5 minutes | 🕐 10 minutes

Busy Morning Breakfast Cupcakes

Quickly baked in a muffin pan, these egg and sausage cupcakes are actually mini quiches. Easily eaten out of hand, these breakfast cakes provide a protein-packed start for a hectic day.

4 ounces Jimmy Dean Pork Maple Sausage
½ cup chopped sweet onions, like Vidalia
½ cup chopped roasted red peppers
(from a jar)
6 large eggs

½ cup heavy whipping cream
½ teaspoon hot sauce
1 (12-ounce) package Pillsbury Golden
Layers Honey Butter Biscuits
1½ cups shredded mild cheddar cheese

Preheat oven to 400°F. Brown sausage and onions in a medium nonstick skillet over medium heat, about 3 minutes, stirring and breaking up the sausage into bite-size pieces. Remove from heat and drain fat. Stir in red peppers.

Place eggs in a medium bowl. Beat with a wire whisk. Whisk in cream and hot sauce.

Coat a 12-count muffin pan with vegetable cooking spray. Divide each of 6 biscuits in half, horizontally, and place one half in the bottom of each muffin cup. (Press dough so that it completely covers the bottom.)

Divide 1 cup cheese among the 12 cups. Divide sausage mixture among cups and place atop cheese. Pour egg batter equally among the cups (about 2 ounces per). Sprinkle remaining cheese atop egg mixture.

Bake for 10–12 minutes, until eggs are set and a wooden skewer inserted in the center of one cupcake comes out clean. Remove pan from oven and run a small, firm, plastic spatula around edges of each cupcake. Then gently place tip of spatula under each one and remove it from the muffin cup.

 Serve 1 cupcake per person for a light breakfast, 2 for a hearty breakfast. You can refrigerate leftover cupcakes and reheat, wrapped in aluminum foil, for 15 minutes in a 325°F oven.

You'll have a half package of biscuits left over, so if you want to double the egg and sausage mixtures and the amount of cheese, you can make a double batch and freeze half for up to 1 month. To reheat: Wrap frozen cupcakes loosely in aluminum foil and place in a 325°F oven for 30 minutes.

Makes: 12 breakfast cupcakes | 20 minutes | 10–12 minutes

Southwestern Scrambled EggBeaters Rollup

This is my own personal start-the-day comfort food. Paired with some cut-up cantaloupe or fresh strawberries, I've got all my food groups covered.

⅓ cup Southwestern-style EggBeaters
Freshly ground black pepper
1 (10-inch) burrito-size flour tortilla
⅓ cup Mexican-style shredded cheese
¼ cup chopped fresh tomato

Place a small nonstick skillet over medium-low heat. Coat skillet with olive oil spray. Add EggBeaters and freshly ground black pepper to taste. Remove skillet from heat just as the EggBeaters begin to set. Stir eggs to scramble until set.

Meanwhile, spread all but 1 tablespoon cheese evenly over tortilla. Microwave tortilla for 20 seconds.

Place EggBeaters on lower third of tortilla. Sprinkle with chopped tomato and the remaining shredded cheese. Fold in right and left sides of tortilla, then fold lower third of tortilla over mixture and continue rolling and folding edges until rollup is formed. Microwave rollup for 15 seconds. Slice in half on the diagonal.

 If you are making these breakfast rollups for several people, you can skip the step of melting the cheese while softening the tortillas. Simply stack up to 4 tortillas and micro-wave them for about 20 seconds, until pliable. Then sprinkle cheese on warm tortillas and proceed with recipe, but increase final microwave time to 20 seconds.

Crumble leftover bacon or thinly slice leftover breakfast sausage links and add to the rollup if you'd like. Or use any unflavored egg substitute and get creative with your own season-ings and fillings.

Serves: 1 | 🍲 2 minutes | ⏱ 5 minutes

Ham-Artichoke-Tomato Frittata

A frittata is actually an Italian omelet loaded with an assortment of savory ingredients. It is not folded over, like a traditional French omelet; instead, it is cooked slowly on the stove, then finished in the oven. Versatile in every way, frittatas are great for breakfast, brunch, lunch, or supper, and can be eaten hot, at room temperature, or even cold.

1 tablespoon canola oil

½ cup diced ham

¼ cup chopped sweet onions, like Vidalia

½ cup chopped jarred marinated artichoke hearts

¼ cup sliced grape tomatoes

6 eggs, beaten

½ cup shredded mild cheddar cheese

2 tablespoons finely snipped fresh basil or 2 teaspoons dried

Preheat oven to 350°F. Heat oil in a 10-inch nonstick ovenproof skillet over medium heat. Add ham and onions and sauté for 30 seconds, stirring constantly. Add artichoke hearts and tomatoes and cook for 30 seconds more, stirring constantly. Reduce heat to low. Pour beaten eggs evenly over filling ingredients. Sprinkle cheese and basil atop egg mixture.

Slowly cook frittata for about 13 minutes, or until the eggs have firmed up around the perimeter and only the center is still slightly runny. Transfer skillet to oven and bake until center has just set, 3–5 minutes more. (Eggs will continue to set up when frittata is removed from the oven.)

Using a firm spatula, transfer frittata to a large cutting board. Cut frittata into thirds.

 When filling a frittata, ingredient possibilities are limited only by your imagination. Follow the simple formula in the recipe above and you can design your own creation. For a 10-inch frittata that generously serves 3, heartily serves 2, or conservatively serves 4, you'll need: 1 tablespoon oil, 6 eggs, 2 cups filling ingredients (in total), and 2 tablespoons freshly snipped herbs or 2 teaspoons dried herbs. Serve the frittata topped with a dollop of sour cream or salsa, or a sprinkle of freshly grated Parmesan cheese, or place frittata on a bed of baby greens dressed with your favorite vinaigrette.

Be sure to prepare all your ingredients before you start cooking the frittata. It goes together very quickly.

Serves: 3 | 🍳 12 minutes | ⏰ 16–18 minutes

Potato Pancakes

I can still see my grandma peeling potatoes and onions at our Wisconsin cabin, while my grandpa sat at the table grating them all by hand into a big bowl. Grandma made her potato pancakes one at a time, the size of the skillet. We all were required to be on deck when it came our turn to eat. You can bet we stood in line!

2 very large or 4 small Yukon Gold potatoes
½ large sweet onion, like Vidalia
1 egg
1 teaspoon salt
2 tablespoons flour
4 tablespoons margarine, divided

Preheat oven to 250°F. Place a nonstick baking sheet on middle rack.

Grate potatoes and onion into the bowl of a food processor. Place grated mixture in a strainer and press on potatoes with the back of a spoon to drain excess liquid. Place chopping blade in processor; add grated potatoes and onion, egg, salt, and flour. Pulse just until mixture is combined. Transfer mixture to a medium bowl.

Melt 2 tablespoons margarine in a large nonstick skillet over medium heat. Add 3 half-cup measures of potato mixture to skillet, placing well apart. Flatten mixture with a firm spatula. Cook potato pancakes for 3 minutes, until browned on the underside. Then flip pancakes and cook 2 minutes more. Transfer pancakes to baking sheet in oven to keep them warm while you cook the second batch of pancakes.

Repeat process with remaining potato pancake batter. Serve immediately.

 Serve pancakes with butter, applesauce, and/or sour cream.

Makes: 6 pancakes | 15–20 minutes | 10 minutes

Apple-Sausage Puffed Pancake

This puffy, baked, German-style pancake is commonly called a Dutch Baby in the United States. It deflates when you take it out of the oven. The pancake batter comes together in a mere 5 minutes. While the pancake bakes, you are free to prepare the savory topping.

2 tablespoons butter, divided
½ cup flour
½ cup milk
2 large eggs, beaten
3 tablespoons plus 2 teaspoons sugar
½ teaspoon vanilla

Dash of salt
3–4 ounces spicy pork sausage
1 cup chopped sweet onions, like Vidalia
2 large sweet-tart apples, like Fuji or Gala, cored, peeled, and cut into ½-inch dice
1 tablespoon confectioners' sugar

Preheat oven to 425°F. Place I tablespoon butter in a 10-inch glass pie plate. Place pie plate on middle rack in oven to melt butter.

Whisk flour and milk together in a medium bowl. Add eggs, 3 tablespoons sugar, vanilla, and salt. Whisk to combine. Pour atop melted butter in pie plate. (Do not mix batter into butter.) Return plate to oven and bake 15–18 minutes, until pancake is puffed and golden.

While pancake is baking, cook sausage in a large nonstick skillet over medium heat until cooked through, stirring frequently to break sausage into bits, about 3 minutes. Remove sausage with a slotted spoon to paper toweling to drain. Add onions to skillet and sauté for 4 minutes, until soft and slightly browned. Remove to a small plate with a slotted spoon.

Melt remaining I tablespoon butter in skillet. Add apples and sprinkle with 2 teaspoons sugar. Sauté until softened but still crisp, about 2 minutes. Reduce heat to low. Return sausage and onions to skillet and stir to combine. Cook, stirring frequently, until mixture is heated through, about 2 minutes.

When the pancake is done, remove it from the oven.

To serve: Cut puffed pancake into quarters. Transfer I wedge to each of 4 plates. Top each portion with one-quarter of the apple-sausage mixture. Sprinkle each portion with confectioners' sugar. Serve immediately.

Make individual puffed pancakes by dividing the pancake batter among four 6-inch, low-sided ovenproof dishes. Melt ¼ tablespoon butter in each dish before adding batter. If you prefer sweet pancake toppings instead of savory, top each portion with sweetened berries or sliced peaches. Finish with a dollop of whipped cream or a drizzle of maple syrup.

Serves: 4 | 10 minutes | 15–18 minutes

Bacon–Four-Cheese Waffles

Celebrate International Waffle Day, March 25, with these savory European-style waffles. The holiday originated in Sweden, the waffle-fest marking the beginning of spring.

8 slices bacon

1 large egg

1 cup sour cream

1 cup whole milk

1 tablespoon butter, melted

2 cups Bisquick

1 cup 4-Cheese Mexican shredded cheese

1 tablespoon confectioners' sugar

Preheat oven to 325°F. Place a pizza pan with perforated holes or a baking sheet on middle oven rack. Preheat waffle iron.

Cook bacon in a large nonstick skillet over medium heat until crispy. Drain on paper toweling and crumble.

While bacon is cooking, beat egg with whisk in a medium bowl. Whisk in sour cream, milk, and butter. Whisk in Bisquick, bacon, and cheese. Mix well.

Using a ½-cup measure (or measure recommended by your waffle iron manufacturer), place batter in center of waffle iron. Close lid and cook until indicator light shows waffle is done. Transfer waffle to heated tray in oven. Repeat process until all waffles are cooked.

To serve: Place confectioners' sugar in a small sieve or shaker. Sprinkle each waffle with confectioners' sugar and serve immediately.

 Serve waffles with maple syrup and/or fresh blueberries, strawberries, or raspberries. You can substitute finely diced ham or Canadian bacon for the crispy bacon and shredded sharp cheddar, gouda, or Swiss for the Mexican cheese blend.

Serves: 4–6 | 15 minutes | 15 minutes

Stuffed Orange French Toast

Some say one can't be too thin or too rich, but this one is too rich to be thin. Cream cheese and orange marmalade are stuffed between two slices of orange-drenched cinnamon-raisin bread and sumptuous flavor infuses every bite.

3 eggs	1 (8-ounce) package whipped cream cheese
¼ cup milk	½ cup orange marmalade
¾ cup orange juice	4 tablespoons (½ stick) butter
1 teaspoon vanilla	Confectioners' sugar (optional)
12 slices cinnamon-raisin bread	Orange slices (optional)

Preheat oven to 220°F. Place eggs, milk, orange juice, and vanilla in a large shallow bowl. Beat mixture with a wire whisk until smooth and frothy.

Spread a thick layer of cream cheese on 6 slices of bread. Spread a layer of orange marmalade on the remaining 6 slices. Top cream cheese slices with orange marmalade slices, to form 6 cream cheese–marmalade sandwiches.

Melt 2 tablespoons butter in a large nonstick skillet over medium-low heat. Dip both sides of 3 sandwiches in the egg mixture and place in skillet. Cook for about 2 minutes, until browned on underside. Flip sandwiches and brown the other side of each sandwich, about 2 minutes more. Remove sandwiches to an oven-safe platter and place in warm oven.

Repeat process, dipping remaining 3 sandwiches in egg mixture, adding remaining 2 tablespoons butter to skillet, and cooking sandwiches until browned on both sides.

To serve: Cut stuffed French toast on the diagonal. Sprinkle with powdered sugar and garnish with orange slices, if desired.

 To serve 2–3 people, cut recipe in half: 6 slices bread, 1 egg plus 1 egg white, 2 tablespoons milk, ¼ cup plus 2 tablespoons orange juice, ½ teaspoon vanilla, 4 ounces whipped cream cheese, ¼ cup marmalade, 2 tablespoons butter.

Serves: 4–6 | 10 minutes | 10 minutes

Loaded Oatmeal Mix

We all know that the best part of oatmeal is all the "stuff" we put on top of it. This master recipe loads the oatmeal with nuts and dried fruits. Use it to make Stovetop Oatmeal, or try the Baked Oatmeal creation (opposite).

4 cups Quaker Old-Fashioned Oats (not quick-cooking)
¼ cup chopped walnuts
½ cup sliced almonds
¼ cup roasted sunflower seeds
¼ cup dried cherries
¼ cup dried cranberries
¼ cup chopped dates
¼ cup chopped dried apricots
1 teaspoon ground cinnamon

Mix all ingredients together in a large bowl. Transfer to an airtight, covered container and keep in pantry until needed, up to 3 months.

 Substitute any of your favorite nuts and dried fruits in this recipe.

Makes: 6 cups | 10 minutes

STOVETOP OATMEAL

In Scotland, oatmeal is served in one bowl, milk in another. Diners dip each spoonful of hot oatmeal in the cold milk, therefore keeping the milk from cooling off the oatmeal.

....

1¼ cup Loaded Oatmeal Mix

Milk or half-and-half

Brown sugar

Place 2 cups water in a medium saucepan over high heat. When water has come to a boil, add 1¼ cups Loaded Oatmeal Mix. Reduce heat to low and cook, uncovered, stirring occasionally, 12 minutes, until water is absorbed. Cover and allow oatmeal to rest for 2 minutes. Serve oatmeal with milk or half-and-half. Sprinkle with brown sugar to taste.

Serves 3–4 | 2 minutes | 16 minutes

BAKED OATMEAL

Not exactly a cake, not quite a cookie, this concoction takes oatmeal to a new level.

....

1⅓ cups Loaded Oatmeal Mix

½ cup milk

½ cup apple juice

¼ cup brown sugar

1 teaspoon vanilla

1 egg, beaten

1 teaspoon baking powder

Milk or half-and-half

Preheat oven to 350°F. Coat a pie plate with vegetable cooking spray.

Place all ingredients in a large bowl and stir to combine. Pour mixture into pie plate. Bake for 20–25 minutes, until oatmeal is almost set. Remove from oven and allow oatmeal to rest for 5 minutes. Serve each portion with milk or half-and-half. (Reheat leftover oatmeal in the oven or microwave.)

Serves 4–6 | 4½ minutes | 20-25 minutes

Out of Hand

• Sandwiches, Pizza, Burgers, and Brats •

Turkey Taco Melts

Grilled P, B, & J

Sloppy Joes

Grilled Five-Cheese Sandwiches

Hot Super Sub

Burger Mania

Sheboygan-style Beer Bratwurst

Meatball Hoagies

Panini, Panini, Panini

VeggiePlus Pizza

Turkey Taco Melts

Unlike the traditional method of each diner assembling his or her own taco from an array of ingredients, these tacos are prepared by the cook and popped in the oven to melt the cheese. Every night that my husband had to work late, my kids asked for tacos, our favorite "no-dad" comfort food. I hold the taco-eating record in our family to this day — seven at one sitting!!

1 teaspoon canola oil
1 pound ground turkey
1 (1.25-ounce) package taco seasoning mix
1 (12-count) package taco shells
1 large tomato

1 large wedge iceberg lettuce
½ sweet onion, like Vidalia
1 (8-ounce) package shredded Mexican or taco cheese
Hot sauce

Preheat oven to 325°F. Heat canola oil in a large nonstick skillet over medium heat. Add ground turkey and cook, stirring frequently, to break up the turkey into bits. Drain on paper toweling, then return ground turkey to skillet. Add taco seasoning and ¾ cup water. Stir to combine. Reduce heat to low and simmer, stirring occasionally, for 5–10 minutes, until liquid is absorbed.

Meanwhile, place taco shells in a 7x11-inch baking dish and place in oven to heat, about 5 minutes. Chop tomato, lettuce, and onion, and place each in a small bowl.

Remove taco shells from oven and place on heatproof pad on counter. Remove skillet from the burner and place on heatproof pad on counter. Assemble each taco as follows: 1 tablespoon taco meat, sprinkling of onions, tomatoes, lettuce. Pack shredded cheese firmly on top (be careful not to break shell) and replace taco in baking dish. Repeat with remaining tacos. Place baking dish back in oven for 5 minutes more, until cheese is melted. Serve immediately with hot sauce.

 You can make a taco salad from these ingredients. Increase the amounts of lettuce, tomatoes, and onions. Add avocado and prepared salsa, if you like. Serve in a prepared tortilla shell.

Serves: 6 (2 tacos per serving) | 25 minutes | 5 minutes

Grilled P, B, & J

You might want to wear a bib for this sandwich — it is so oozingly rich and peanut-buttery. Elevating the old classic to new heights, this hot peanut butter and jelly sandwich will lift your spirits any time of day or night.

1 heaping kitchenware tablespoon peanut butter
1 heaping kitchenware tablespoon jelly or jam
2 thick slices of bread
Soft butter or margarine

Mix peanut butter and jelly together in a small bowl. Spread mixture evenly atop 1 slice bread. Place second slice bread atop peanut butter mixture to make a sandwich. Spread top and bottom of sandwich with butter or margarine. Place in a nonstick skillet over medium-low heat. Cook until underside is golden, about 3 minutes. Flip sandwich and cook until underside is golden, about 1½ minutes more. Remove from heat, cut sandwich in half, and serve immediately.

Combining the peanut butter and jelly keeps the jelly from soaking into the bread. You can experiment with your choice of chunky or smooth peanut butter and any jams, jellies, or preserves that you like. For an adult twist, try cashew butter or almond butter instead of the peanut butter and substitute a more savory flavor, like chutney, for the jam.

Serves: 1 | 3 minutes | 4½ minutes

Sloppy Joes

The smoky flavor of these sandwiches conjures visions of a Southern smokehouse. You'll never reach for Manwich again.

1 teaspoon olive oil
1 pound ground beef
½ cup chopped celery
½ cup chopped sweet onions, like Vidalia
1 (8-ounce) can tomato sauce
½ cup ketchup
3 tablespoons smoky barbecue sauce, like Sweet Baby Ray's

1 tablespoon honey mustard
1 tablespoon brown sugar
1 tablespoon Worcestershire sauce
1 tablespoon white vinegar
Kosher salt and cracked pepper
1 (6-count) package hamburger buns
6 slices Swiss cheese

Warm oil in a large nonstick skillet over medium heat. Add ground beef, celery, and onions and sauté, stirring frequently to break up the beef, for 7 minutes, or until beef is browned. Drain beef mixture in a colander, then return it to skillet.

Reduce heat to low. Add tomato sauce, ketchup, barbecue sauce, honey mustard, brown sugar, Worcestershire sauce, and vinegar. Stir to combine. Add a pinch of salt and pepper.

Simmer, uncovered, stirring occasionally, for 15 minutes. Serve in toasted hamburger buns, each topped with a slice of Swiss cheese.

If you don't like the smoky taste of the barbecue sauce, substitute a lighter barbecue sauce, like Open Pit or Kraft, and reduce ketchup to ¼ cup.

Serves: 6 | 8 minutes | 22 minutes

Grilled Five-Cheese Sandwiches

My mother always called grilled cheese sandwiches "cheese toastwiches," which as a child I thought were very special. This version redefines the classic, following the self-indulgent concept that, like chocolate and jewelry, one can never have too much cheese.

1 cup shredded cheddar cheese
1 cup shredded Monterey Jack cheese
1 cup shredded Swiss cheese
1 (3-ounce) package cream cheese, softened
¼ cup mayonnaise
¼ teaspoon garlic powder

2 teaspoons Dijon mustard
2 slices white, sourdough, or whole-grain bread (per serving)
1 tablespoon salted butter, room temperature
1 tablespoon Parmesan cheese

Mix together cheddar, jack, Swiss, and cream cheeses in a medium bowl. Add mayonnaise, garlic powder, and mustard. Stir until ingredients are well mixed.

For each sandwich: Spread about ¼ cup cheese filling atop 1 slice bread. Top with another slice bread. Butter both sides of the sandwich. Sprinkle each with Parmesan cheese.

Place a nonstick skillet over medium-low heat for 30 seconds. Place sandwich in skillet and cook for 3 minutes. Flip sandwich with a firm spatula. Cook for 1½ minutes, until golden brown. Flip sandwich one more time, press down on sandwich with spatula, and cook for 30 seconds longer. Remove sandwich from skillet, cut it on the diagonal, and serve immediately.

The cooking directions are for making 1 sandwich. The actual cheese filling will make 10 sandwiches. You can refrigerate filling in a covered container for up to 1 month. Be sure to cook sandwich on medium-low heat, so that cheese has a chance to melt before bread gets too browned.

Cheese Filling Makes: 10 sandwiches | 10 minutes | 5 minutes

Hot Super Sub

Italian immigrants to America made a traditional sandwich consisting of a long loaf of bread filled with cold cuts and topped with a salad of lettuce, tomatoes, onions, olive oil, vinegar, salt, pepper, and Italian spices. A New York City grocer, who sold the sandwiches in 1910, reportedly named them submarines because the shape of the bread reminded him of naval subs.

4 tablespoons (½ stick) butter, room temperature

1 tablespoon Dijon mustard

1 tablespoon snipped fresh parsley or ½ teaspoon dried

1 large clove garlic, crushed and minced

¼ teaspoon crushed red pepper flakes

1 loaf Italian bread, sliced in half lengthwise

¼ pound thinly sliced deli ham

¼ pound thinly sliced salami

¼ pound thinly sliced large pepperoni

1 medium sweet onion, like Vidalia, thinly sliced

1 (12-ounce) jar mild banana pepper rings

2 medium tomatoes, thinly sliced

6 ounces Muenster cheese, thinly sliced

Preheat oven to 400°F. Combine butter, mustard, parsley, garlic, and red pepper flakes in a small bowl. Spread entire butter mixture on cut sides of top and bottom of bread. On bottom slice of bread, layer ingredients — ham, salami, pepperoni, onions, pepper rings, tomatoes, cheese — in order. Put top half of bread over ingredients, forming a sandwich. Wrap tightly in several layers of aluminum foil. Place on a baking sheet and bake for 20–25 minutes, until cheese melts. Cut into 6–8 pieces and serve hot.

 If you keep the baked sandwich wrapped in several layers of foil and then wrap it in a dish towel, it will stay hot for a couple of hours. This is great fare for the beach, boat, or a picnic. You can substitute any of your favorite cold cuts for the salami, ham, and pepperoni. If you would like to add a spicy jolt to your sandwich, substitute hot pepper rings for the mild banana peppers.

Serves: 6–8 | 🍲 10 minutes | 🕐 20–25 minutes

Burger Mania

Baby burgers, commonly called "sliders" in some restaurants, are increasingly popular on the American burger scene. I've taken these mini burgers one step further, by seasoning them from the inside, not the outside, in three different ways: Portobello, Onion, and Swiss; Blue Cheese; and Cheddar and Bacon. With this platter of little burgers, you can enjoy a taste of each.

2½ pounds ground beef (90 percent lean)

2 slices bacon, cut into small dice

⅓ cup finely chopped portobello mushrooms

¼ cup finely chopped sweet onions, like Vidalia

¼ cup shredded Swiss cheese

⅓ cup crumbled blue cheese

⅓ cup shredded cheddar cheese

Salt and freshly ground black pepper

1 (15-count) package White Dollar Rolls or other 3-inch-diameter round rolls

Divide ground beef into 3 equal portions and place in separate medium bowls. Cook bacon in a medium nonstick skillet over medium heat until bacon is cooked through but not crispy. Remove from heat and drain. While bacon is cooking, chop mushrooms and onions. Mix mushrooms, onions, and Swiss cheese with ground beef in one bowl. Mix blue cheese with ground beef in second bowl. Mix bacon and cheddar cheese with ground beef in third bowl.

Using a 3-inch-diameter round biscuit ring, form burger patties with your clean hands. Divide beef mixture in each bowl into 4 equal portions. Press beef into ring to form a patty that is 1 inch thick. Repeat with beef mixtures in the two remaining bowls. (You'll have 12 patties, 4 of each variety, 3 inches in diameter and 1 inch thick.) Season burgers with salt and freshly ground black pepper to taste.

Preheat outdoor grill to 475°F. Cut rolls in half, horizontally. Place burgers on hot grill. Cook burgers for about 4 minutes. Flip burgers and cook 4 minutes more for medium-rare. Check doneness by cutting into one burger with a knife. Adjust timing for rare or medium burgers. Toast buns briefly on grill rack before serving. Serve burgers with sliced Roma tomatoes and baby lettuce, along with traditional burger condiments.

 You'll need a 3-inch-diameter round biscuit ring or cookie cutter. You can find White Dollar Rolls at Walmart Superstores. They are baked fresh every day and are the perfect miniature burger bun size. If you don't have access to this store, substitute another 3-inch-diameter round roll. Create your own filling combinations. Form the beef mixtures into conventional-size burgers if you wish.

Serves: 6 (2 miniature burgers per serving) | 20 minutes | 8 minutes

Sheboygan-style Beer Bratwurst

Long considered Wisconsin's soul food, bratwurst Sheboygan style sets the gold standard. These folks take their brats seriously, and hold to a couple of hard and fast rules: Never boil a bratwurst — lightly simmer it in beer and onions. Never serve bratwurst in a hot dog bun — use brat buns, which are slightly larger and chewier. And never, ever put yellow mustard on a bratwurst — use a brown German-style mustard instead.

1 large sweet onion, like Vidalia

1 (5-count) package Original Flavor Johnsonville Bratwurst

1 bottle beer

1 (5-count) package brat buns or hard rolls, cut in half horizontally

Cut onion into thin slices. Chop several slices to make 1 cup. Place chopped onions in a zipper bag and refrigerate until needed.

Place bratwurst in a large saucepan. Place sliced onions atop bratwurst. Pour beer over brats. Fill beer bottle twice with water and pour the water over the brats. Simmer the brats over low heat for 10 minutes, until they plump up and have a milky-looking exterior. Do not boil.

Preheat outdoor grill to hot. Using tongs, remove brats from beer and onion mixture; reserve mixture. Place bratwurst on grill for 4–5 minutes, until underside is golden, without being burned. (Never pierce bratwurst with a fork; they will lose their juices.) Turn brats with tongs and cook 3–4 minutes longer, until underside is golden. (Don't allow the brats to split or get too black or they will dry out.)

Serve bratwurst immediately or return brats to simmering beer and onion mixture (low heat) until ready to serve. (You can keep them warm in the beer mixture for up to 1 hour.) Toast buns briefly on grill rack before serving.

To serve: Serve brats on buns. In Sheboygan, brats are traditionally served with "the works," a choice of chopped onions, mustard, ketchup, and pickles. Purists believe adding sauerkraut is an abomination.

To do brats for a crowd, double or triple this recipe. Grill them ahead of time and serve them in a large pot of slightly simmering beer and onions. Keep extra brats warm in the beer mixture until people are ready for another. The simmering beer keeps the sausages moist.

Makes: 5 | 15 minutes | 8–10 minutes

Meatball Hoagies

This is the ultimate recycled meal. Use surplus meatballs from Spaghetti and Neapolitan Meatballs recipe (see recipe page 50). Hot and hearty, these sandwiches are perfect for a cold winter day . . . or night.

8 Neapolitan Meatballs
1½ cups prepared pasta sauce
4 (7-inch) bolillo or hoagie rolls
Olive oil spray
4 slices mozzarella cheese, cut about 5 inches long and ¼-inch thick
Parmesan cheese

Preheat oven to 400°F. Place meatballs and sauce in a large saucepan over medium heat and cook until warmed through, about 10 minutes.

Meanwhile, slice tops off rolls and discard. Pull the bread out of the rolls to form bread shells about ½-inch thick. Coat inside of bread shells with olive oil spray. Place a slice of mozzarella cheese in each shell. Place shells on a baking sheet and bake until cheese melts and shell is crisp, about 7 minutes.

To assemble: Put a layer of sauce in the bottom of each shell. Top each with 2 meatballs. Drizzle sauce over meatballs and sprinkle each serving with Parmesan cheese.

 The Neapolitan-style Meatballs recipe (page 50) makes 74 meatballs, more than enough for both a spaghetti dinner and meatball sandwiches. Use your favorite prepared pasta sauce or leftover spaghetti sauce for the hoagies.

Serves: 4 | 10 minutes | 🕐 7 minutes

Panini, Panini, Panini

The panini — meaning "little breads" in Italian — is a formulaic creation with endless possibilities. Start with great artisan bread, like ciabatta, readily available in supermarkets these days. Use a couple of highly flavored spreads sparingly, and fill the panini with a scant combination of the meats, cheeses, and veggies of your choice. No need for a panini press — use a George Foreman–style electric grill instead. If you don't have one, place sandwich in a skillet over medium heat. Place another skillet atop sandwich and weight it down with an extra-large can of stewed tomatoes.

TUNA-ARTICHOKE PANINI
The tuna melt gets a makeover.

1 (6-ounce) can white tuna in water, drained
¼ cup prepared artichoke tapenade or chopped marinated artichokes
3 tablespoons mayonnaise
2 tablespoons chopped sweet onions, like Vidalia
½ teaspoon lemon juice
¼ teaspoon salt
⅛ teaspoon pepper
2 (¾–1-inch-thick) slices crusty artisan bread (per sandwich)
Olive oil spray
2 slices baby Swiss cheese (per sandwich)

Preheat George Foreman–style grill. Mix tuna, artichoke tapenade, mayonnaise, onions, lemon juice, salt, and pepper together in a medium bowl. Using a Misto or other olive oil spray bottle, thoroughly coat one side of each bread slice with olive oil. Turn slices over. Place one slice cheese atop each bread slice. Spread ¼ cup tuna mixture atop one cheese slice. Put halves together to form a sandwich. Place sandwich on grill and close lid. Cook for 4½ minutes, until bread is golden brown, tuna has heated through, and cheese has melted. Serve immediately.

 This tuna mixture makes enough filling for 4 panini sandwiches. Use 2 slices bread and 2 slices cheese for each sandwich. Refrigerate unused mixture in a covered container for up to 5 days.

Makes: 1 panini | 7½ minutes | 4½ minutes

SMOKED TURKEY AND SPINACH PANINI

Not just a turkey sandwich . . .

....

2 slices ciabatta or other artisan bread

1 tablespoon prepared cranberry relish

1 slice Swiss cheese

1 teaspoon prepared horseradish sauce

1 ounce thin-sliced smoked turkey

Handful fresh baby spinach leaves

Preheat George Foreman–style grill. Using a Misto or other olive oil spray bottle, thoroughly coat one side of each bread slice with olive oil. Turn slices over. Spread cranberry relish on one bread slice. Top with cheese. Spread horseradish sauce over other bread slice. Top with smoked turkey. Place spinach leaves atop turkey. Put halves together to form a sandwich.

Place sandwich on grill and close lid. Cook for 2 minutes, until bread is golden brown and cheese has melted. Serve immediately.

Makes I panini | 4½ minutes | 2 minutes

PANINI CAPRESE

The popular tomato-mozzarella-basil salad goes panini.

....

2 slices ciabatta or other artisan bread

2 teaspoons basil pesto

2 slices mozzarella cheese,
    cut ¼-inch thick

2 slices tomato, cut ¼-inch thick

Salt and black pepper

Preheat George Foreman–style grill. Using a Misto or other olive oil spray bottle, thoroughly coat one side of each bread slice with olive oil. Turn slices over. Place 1 slice mozzarella cheese on each bread slice. Spread pesto on each cheese slice. Place tomato slices on one cheese-topped bread slice. Sprinkle with salt and pepper to taste. Put halves together to form a sandwich. Place sandwich on grill and close lid. Cook for 2 minutes, until bread is golden brown and cheese has melted. Serve immediately.

Makes I panini |  4½ minutes | 2 minutes

VeggiePlus Pizza

Sunday night is often pizza night at our house. Veggie pizzas are my personal favorites, but my husband prefers a meatier version. So I divide packages of hot sausage, hamburger, pepperoni, and ham into 4-ounce portions and freeze them. When Sunday rolls around, I simply defrost a meat portion and add it to his half of the pizza. I have to confess, spicy pork sausage often finds itself sprinkled on my half as well (see *below).*

1 (12-inch) Mama Mary's Gourmet Pizza Thin & Crispy Crust
¾ cup sweet basil pasta sauce
¼ chopped sweet onions, like Vidalia
⅓ cup sliced fresh mushrooms
¼ cup diced green, red, or yellow bell peppers
⅓ cup chopped tomatoes
1 tablespoon pine nuts
2 tablespoons raisins
1 (8-ounce) package Pizza! Shredded Mozzarella & Cheddar Cheese

Preheat oven to 450°F. Place pizza crust on a pizza pan (preferably with holes) or a baking sheet. Spread pasta sauce over crust, leaving a ½-inch rim of crust around edges. Sprinkle onions, mushrooms, peppers, tomatoes, pine nuts, and raisins over pizza. Top with shredded cheese.

Reduce oven temperature to 425°F. Bake for 8 minutes, until cheese is melted and crust is golden.

 For a spicy, meaty pizza, sauté 4 ounces hot pork sausage in a medium nonstick skillet over medium heat, breaking up sausage with a wooden spoon. When sausage is cooked through, about 3 minutes, drain on paper toweling. Substitute your favorite pasta sauce and your favorite toppings and/or meats for those mentioned above. For Greek-style pizza, eliminate the pasta sauce and coat crust with olive oil spray.

I have found Mama Mary's prepared pizza crusts to bake up closest to pizza kitchen crusts. (They come in regular, thin, whole wheat, and deep dish.) But you can use Boboli crusts or refrigerated pizza dough if you prefer.

Serves: 4 (2 slices per serving) | 🍽 20 minutes | ⏱ 8 minutes

Some Like It in the Pot

• Soups, Stews, Chili, and Chowders •

Beef and Bean Chili

New England Clam Chowder

Curried Chicken Noodle Soup

Creamy Roasted Tomato Soup

Spinach and Tortellini Soup

Spicy Corn and Shrimp Chowder

Pasta e Fagioli

Asian Vegetable Chicken-Dumpling Soup

Butternut Squash Soup

Slow Cooker Beef Stew

Beef and Bean Chili

Nothing beats a big bowl of chili on an autumn day and this recipe is as easy as it is satisfying. If you prefer a meatless chili, substitute a couple of cans of Great Northern, pinto, or black beans for the ground beef.

1 teaspoon olive oil

1 pound ground beef

½ cup chopped sweet onions, like Vidalia

1 (4.9-ounce) package Bear Creek "Darn Good" Chili Mix

1 (6-ounce) can tomato paste

1 (14.5-ounce) can Petite Cut Diced Tomatoes with Garlic and Olive Oil

1 cup shredded sharp cheddar cheese

Place oil in a large nonstick skillet over medium heat. Add beef and onions and sauté, stirring occasionally, for 3 minutes or until beef is cooked through and crumbly. Drain on paper toweling.

Meanwhile, place 5 cups water in a large soup pot. Bring to a boil over high heat. Add chili mix, tomato paste, and chopped tomatoes. Stir to mix well. Reduce heat to low. Add ground beef and onions and stir to mix. Simmer, uncovered, stirring occasionally, for 20 minutes. Sprinkle each portion with cheddar cheese before serving.

Kick up the heat level in this chili by adding chili or chipotle powder to taste.

Serves: 8 (1½ cups per serving) | 10 minutes | 20 minutes

New England Clam Chowder

In New England making "chowdah" is serious business. Every summer in Newport, Rhode Island, thirty of the nation's top chefs cook up more than 3,000 gallons of chowder during the Great Chowder Cook-off competition.

5 slices bacon, cut into ½-inch dice

2 pounds Yukon Gold potatoes

2 cups chopped sweet onions, like Vidalia

1 teaspoon garlic powder

2 tablespoons flour

4 (6.5-ounce) cans chopped clams, drained and juices reserved

2 (8-ounce) bottles clam juice

1 cup water

1 teaspoon hot sauce

1 cup half-and-half

Fry bacon in a large nonstick soup pot over medium heat, stirring occasionally. While bacon is cooking, peel potatoes and cut them into ½-inch dice. Set aside.

When bacon is nearly cooked through, remove all but about 1 tablespoon bacon grease. (If bacon is particularly lean and you don't have any grease, add 1 tablespoon canola oil.) Add onions and garlic powder. Sauté onions, stirring frequently, until they soften, about 3 minutes. Stir flour into onion mixture.

Stirring constantly, slowly add reserved juice from clams, bottled clam juice, water, and potatoes. Increase temperature to high, and cover pot. When mixture comes to a boil, uncover pot and reduce heat to medium-low. Simmer for 5 minutes, stirring occasionally, until potatoes are cooked through al dente.

Reduce heat to low. Add clams, hot sauce, and half-and-half. Stir to combine ingredients. Simmer for 5 minutes more, until soup has heated through and potatoes are tender.

 For Rhode Island–style clam chowder, which has a clear broth, do not add the half-and-half. For the red-based Manhattan-style chowder, replace the half-and-half with a (14.5-ounce) can of diced tomatoes with juices or 1 cup tomato juice.

Serves: 6 (1½ cups per serving) | 12 minutes | 18 minutes

Curried Chicken Noodle Soup

A steaming bowl of chicken noodle soup spells comfort in any culture, it seems. This hearty supper recipe adds the distinctive Indian flavors of curry and ginger, along with crunchy tart apples and sweet raisins, for a decidedly global twist on the original.

1 (9.3-ounce) package Bear Creek Chicken Noodle Soup Mix

2 teaspoons Sharwood's or Madras mild curry powder

1 teaspoon gingerroot paste or minced fresh gingerroot

¼ teaspoon dried crushed red pepper (optional)

1 (14.5-ounce) can Petite Cut Diced Tomatoes with Garlic and Olive Oil, with juices

1 store-bought rotisserie chicken, cut into bite-size pieces (about 4 cups)

¼ cup currants or raisins

2 cups peeled and diced tart apple

Place 8 cups water in a large covered soup pot over high heat. When water comes to a rolling boil, add soup mix, curry powder, gingerroot, and optional crushed red pepper. Stir to combine ingredients. Reduce heat to medium and cook, stirring constantly, for 1 minute. Reduce heat to low and add tomatoes, chicken, and currants. Simmer 10 minutes, uncovered. Stir in apples, heat for 1 minute, and serve.

 You'll find a variety of Gourmet Garden's herb pastes in the produce section of your supermarket — gingerroot, garlic, red chili pepper, cilantro, basil, lemongrass, and more. They save an enormous amount of time, eliminating tedious prep work, and have a long refrigerator life.

If you are a curry lover, feel free to add another teaspoon. If you hate curry, simply eliminate the spice from this recipe.

Serves: 8 (1½ cups per serving) | 10 minutes | 🕐 15 minutes

Creamy Roasted Tomato Soup

Hunt's Fire Roasted Diced Tomatoes are a recent addition to the canned tomato market. As you might expect, their flavor is slightly sweeter and less acidic than that of regular canned tomatoes.

2 (14.5-ounce) cans Hunt's Fire Roasted
   Diced Tomatoes
½ teaspoon baking soda
4 tablespoons (½ stick) butter
½ cup finely chopped sweet onions,
   like Vidalia
¼ cup flour

2 cups whole milk
2 cups College Inn White Wine & Herb
   Culinary Broth
1 tablespoon honey
1½ teaspoons salt
1 teaspoon dried basil
Snipped fresh basil (optional)

Place tomatoes and baking soda in a blender and pulse until tomatoes are pureed. Set aside.

Melt butter in a large soup pot over medium heat. Add onions and cook, stirring frequently, until they are softened but not browned, about 1½ minutes. Sprinkle flour over onions and stir to combine, cooking about 30 seconds. Stirring constantly, slowly add milk, broth, honey, salt, and dried basil. Continue cooking and stirring until mixture has thickened slightly, about 5 minutes. Stir in pureed tomatoes.

Place soup in blender, a half batch at a time. Puree until smooth. Return soup to pot, reduce heat to low, and cook for 3 minutes, stirring frequently. Serve each portion with a sprinkling of fresh basil.

 If you prefer your tomato soup "rustico," peppered with chewy bits of onion and tomato, skip the final blender puree step. You can substitute any kind of diced tomatoes for the roasted variety, but you may need to adjust seasonings to taste. You can substitute vegetable broth for the specialty broth above; just add a splash of white wine and a pinch of thyme and rosemary to the mix.

Makes: 6 (1½ cups per serving) | 3 minutes | 10 minutes

Spinach and Tortellini Soup

This easy, hearty, healthy soup proves the old adage that sometimes less is more.

1 tablespoon olive oil

2 teaspoons garlic paste or minced garlic

½ cup white wine

1 (32-ounce) carton chicken broth

1 (8.8-ounce) package dried cheese tortellini

1 (14.5-ounce) can Petite Cut Diced Tomatoes, with juices

½ (6-ounce) package baby spinach

Salt and freshly ground black pepper

Parmesan cheese

Heat oil in a large nonstick soup pot over medium heat. Add garlic and sauté, stirring constantly for 30 seconds. Add wine and cook, stirring frequently, for 1 minute. Stir in chicken broth, increase heat to high, cover, and bring to a boil. When liquid has come to a full boil, add tortellini and reduce heat to medium-low. Cover pot and simmer, stirring occasionally, for 12 minutes. Stir in tomatoes and spinach. Reduce heat to low and simmer for 5 minutes more, or until spinach has wilted and tortellini is al dente. Season each portion with salt and freshly ground black pepper to taste and a sprinkling of Parmesan cheese.

 If your supermarket carries College Inn Culinary Broths, substitute White Wine Herb Broth for the plain chicken broth. It is subtly flavored with Chablis wine, thyme, and rosemary and will add an extra zing to the soup.

Serves: 4 (1½ cups per serving) | 5 minutes | 20 minutes

Spicy Corn and Shrimp Chowder

The dark green poblano chile pepper, mild to medium in heat index, adds a spicy richness to this hearty chowder. When dried, these peppers are known as Ancho chilies.

6 slices bacon

1 cup chopped sweet onions, like Vidalia

1 large poblano chile pepper, seeded and chopped

1 large potato, cut into ½-inch dice (about 1½ cups)

2 (14.75-ounce) cans cream-style corn

1 (16-ounce) package frozen corn, thawed

2 (14-ounce) cans chicken broth

2 teaspoons sugar

¼ teaspoon cayenne pepper

1 (4-ounce) can tiny shrimp

1 cup whole milk

Fry bacon in a large nonstick soup pot over medium heat until crispy. Remove bacon to drain on paper toweling. Reserve 2 tablespoons bacon grease in pot. Discard the rest.

Place onions, chilies, and diced potatoes in soup pot and sauté over medium heat, stirring frequently, until vegetables have softened, about 3 minutes. While vegetables are cooking, crumble bacon into bite-size pieces.

Remove pot from heat. Add bacon, canned and frozen corn, chicken broth, sugar, and cayenne pepper. Return pot to burner and increase heat to high. Stir soup, cover pot, and bring to a boil. When soup has come to a full boil, reduce heat to low, uncover pot, and add shrimp. Simmer for 3 minutes. Slowly add milk, stirring constantly. Simmer for 5 minutes more, until milk has heated through and soup is creamy.

 You can substitute bell peppers for the poblano chilies in a pinch. If you do, increase cayenne pepper to ½ teaspoon.

Serves: 6 (1½ cups per serving) | 5 minutes | 🕐 23 minutes

Pasta e Fagioli

Long a staple in Italian peasant households, this hearty, inexpensive pasta and bean soup spells comfort in any language.

4 slices bacon, cut into ½-inch dice

½ cup chopped sweet onions, like Vidalia

3 teaspoons garlic paste or minced garlic

2 cups water

1 cup uncooked pipette, tubetti, ditalini, or other small tube-shaped pasta

½ teaspoon oregano

¼ teaspoon salt

¼ teaspoon black pepper

1 (15-ounce) can crushed tomatoes or tomato puree

12 ounces College Inn Rotisserie Chicken Bold Stock

2 (15.8-ounce) cans Great Northern beans, rinsed and drained

Parmesan cheese

Fry bacon in a large nonstick soup pot over medium heat for 1 minute, stirring frequently. Add onions and garlic and cook for 2 minutes more, stirring frequently. (If bacon is particularly lean, add 1 teaspoon olive oil.) Add water, pasta, oregano, salt, pepper, tomatoes, and chicken stock. Stir to mix well. Bring to a boil, reduce heat to low, and simmer for 5 minutes, stirring occasionally. Stir in beans and cook for 5 minutes more, until pasta is al dente and beans are heated through. Serve each portion topped with a sprinkling of Parmesan cheese.

 College Inn, which has long made quality chicken stock, has come out with a new line of "bold" or "culinary" stocks, which are packed with extra flavor. If you substitute regular chicken stock, adjust seasonings to taste.

Serves: 5 (1½ cups per serving) | 7 minutes | 15 minutes

Asian Vegetable Chicken-Dumpling Soup

This soup is amazing — amazingly fast, amazingly easy, amazingly tasty, amazingly global. The flavors in this dumpling soup, spicy and satisfying, evoke a trip to the Far East.

1 (13-ounce) package frozen Ling Ling Potstickers Vegetable Dumplings
1 (12-ounce) package frozen Birds Eye Asian Medley or other seasoned Asian vegetables
8 ounces white button mushrooms
1 teaspoon canola oil
1 teaspoon gingerroot paste or minced gingerroot
1 teaspoon garlic paste or minced garlic
1 (32-ounce) carton College Inn Culinary Thai Coconut Curry Broth
1 cup water

Place a large water-filled saucepan over high heat and bring to a boil. Add potsticker dumplings and cook for 8 minutes. Remove cooked dumplings to a plate with a slotted spoon. Set aside.

While potstickers are cooking, roughly chop frozen vegetables into bite-size pieces. Set aside. Remove stems from mushrooms and wipe them clean with paper toweling. Slice mushrooms and set aside.

Heat 1 teaspoon canola oil in a large wok or soup pot over medium-high heat. Add gingerroot and garlic, and sauté, stirring constantly, for 1 minute. Add broth and 1 cup water. When broth comes to a boil, reduce heat to medium-low. Add vegetables and mushrooms and cook for 2 minutes. Add cooked potsticker dumplings and heat for 1 minute more.

To serve: Place 2 potsticker dumplings in the bottom of each of 6 flat-bottomed soup bowls. Ladle soup over dumplings.

College Inn Thai Coconut Curry Broth is essential to this recipe. If you can't find it, improvise by adding some coconut milk, a teaspoon of sesame oil, a little extra gingerroot, and a dash or two of red pepper flakes to conventional chicken broth. You can use any brand of potstickers. Follow package instructions for cooking time.

Serves: 6 (1½ cups per serving) | 5 minutes | 12 minutes

Butternut Squash Soup

Butternut squash is so rich and pure that it doesn't need much window dressing to take a starring role at the dinner table. This simple soup allows the squash's sweet, nutty flavor to shine through.

1 tablespoon butter

1 teaspoon garlic paste or minced garlic

½ cup chopped sweet onions, like Vidalia

2 pounds butternut squash, seeded, peeled, and cut into ½-inch dice

1 teaspoon gingerroot paste or minced gingerroot

½ teaspoon salt

⅛ teaspoon black pepper

Dash of allspice

2 cups chicken broth

2 tablespoons sherry (optional)

Sour cream

Melt butter in a large soup pot over medium heat. Add garlic and onions and sauté, stirring frequently, for 2 minutes.

Add squash, gingerroot, salt, pepper, allspice, broth, and sherry. Increase heat to high. Bring to a boil. Reduce heat to low, cover pot, and simmer until squash is fork-tender, about 5 minutes.

Remove from heat and puree with an immersion stick blender or puree in batches in a blender. Return soup to pot. Simmer on low for another minute, or until soup is hot. Serve topped with a dollop of sour cream.

For an even faster preparation, substitute two 20-ounce packages of frozen peeled and cut butternut squash.

Serves: 4 (1½ cups per serving) | 16½ minutes | 12 minutes

Slow Cooker Beef Stew

 |

You can save a few minutes prep time by purchasing already cut-up stew meat, but you won't necessarily know what cut of meat you are getting. Watch for sales or last-day markdowns of rump roast, which is bottom round, at your local supermarket. I think it is a tastier cut.

½ cup flour

1 teaspoon salt

1 teaspoon cracked black pepper

2 to 2½ pounds rump, round, or chuck roast, cut into 1½-inch cubes

5 medium-size Yukon Gold potatoes, quartered and then cut into thirds

1 medium sweet onion, like Vidalia, peeled and cut into eighths

1 (16-ounce) bag baby carrots

10 ounces College Inn Beef Sirloin Bold Stock

1 (14-ounce) can tomato sauce

Place flour, salt, and pepper in a zipper bag. Shake to mix. Add beef, close zipper, and shake until all sides of cubes are coated with flour. Transfer beef and flour to a slow cooker. Add potatoes, onions, and carrots to the slow cooker.

Mix stock and tomatoes together in a medium bowl. Pour mixture over beef and vegetables. Cover slow cooker and cook on low for 8 hours or on high for 4 hours.

 College Inn Beef Sirloin Bold Stock is packed with extra flavor and is already seasoned with herbs and spices. Offered at the same basic price as regular stock, it is almost as good as homemade. You can substitute traditional beef broth, but adjust seasonings to taste.

Serves: 6 | 14 minutes | ⏱ 8 hours

Oodles of Noodles

• Pasta, Pasta, Pasta •

Mac 'n' Jack

Slow Cooker Spinach Lasagna

Chicken Puttanesca

Linguine with Clam Sauce

Spaghetti and Neapolitan-style Meatballs

Chicken Tetrazzini

Slow Cooker Pasta Bolognese

Hamburger Stroganoff

Spaghetti Carbonara

Penne with Fresh Tomato Sauce and Shrimp

Peanut Noodles

Mac 'n' Jack

Baked macaroni and cheese is pure comfort food and to make it right, you just can't rush it. You can, however, make this recipe up to the baking point a day ahead and refrigerate it until needed. Or freeze it (either the entire recipe or divided into two smaller portions), and bake it on another day. Before baking, thaw Mac 'n' Jack and allow it to reach room temperature.

1 pound dried mini penne or elbow macaroni
4 tablespoons (½ stick) butter
3 tablespoons flour
2 cups chicken broth
¼ cup sherry
1 cup heavy cream
1 cup (about 5 ounces) shredded Monterey Jack cheese

½ cup (about 2 ounces) shredded Kraft White Sharp Cheddar, Swiss, & Parmesan Cheese combo
½ cup (about 2 ounces) shredded pepper jack cheese
Salt and freshly ground black pepper
½ cup fresh bread crumbs
¼ cup grated Parmesan cheese

Preheat oven to 375°F. Bring a large pot of water to boil over medium-high heat. Add penne and cook to al dente, following package directions, about 9 minutes. Drain in a colander.

While penne is cooking, melt butter in a large nonstick skillet over medium heat. Stir in flour and cook for about 30 seconds. Gradually pour in chicken broth and sherry, stirring constantly. Stir in cream. When mixture just starts to bubble, remove from heat and stir in the three shredded cheeses. Add penne and stir to mix well. Season with salt and freshly ground black pepper to taste. Transfer to a 9x13-inch or two 8-inch-square baking dishes, which have been coated with vegetable cooking spray.

Place bread crumbs and Parmesan cheese in a small bowl. Stir to mix. Sprinkle crumbs atop macaroni and cheese mixture. Bake for 30 minutes.

 Substitute any combination of your favorite cheeses for those in this recipe. Keeping the same proportions, use 1 cup of your mildest cheese and accent the flavor with the other two. If all your cheeses are fairly bland, add ½ teaspoon of your favorite dried herbs to the cheese sauce.

Serves: 12 (Serves 6 per 8-inch-square dish) | 26 minutes | 30 minutes

Slow Cooker Spinach Lasagna

Controversy abounds over which European country gets credit for inventing lasagna, that most comforting of all comfort foods. As with all good things that have washed ashore here, we have laid claim to this heartening layered dish and made it distinctly American.

1 (14.5-ounce) can Diced Tomatoes with Basil, Garlic, and Oregano, drained

1 (26-ounce) jar marinara sauce

1 (6-ounce) can tomato paste

1 teaspoon olive oil

½ cup chopped sweet onions, like Vidalia

8 ounces button or baby portobello mushrooms, sliced

2 teaspoons minced garlic

1 (16-ounce) bag frozen chopped spinach, slightly thawed

1 (16-ounce) container smooth and creamy cottage cheese

1 (8-ounce) package shredded mozzarella cheese

1 large egg, beaten

½ teaspoon salt

¼ teaspoon pepper

1 (8-ounce) package no-cook flat (not curly edged) lasagna noodles

½ cup grated Parmesan cheese

In a large bowl, mix together diced tomatoes, marinara sauce, and tomato paste. Set aside.

Heat oil in a large nonstick skillet over medium heat. Add onions, mushrooms, and garlic and sauté, stirring frequently, for 3 minutes. Add spinach and sauté, stirring frequently, until liquid has cooked off, about 3 minutes more. Remove from heat and place spinach mixture in a large bowl. Add cottage cheese, shredded mozzarella, egg, salt, and pepper, and stir to mix thoroughly.

Spread 1 cup tomato mixture in the bottom of a slow cooker. Top with a complete covering of lasagna noodles. (Break noodles to fit all spaces, overlapping if necessary.) Spread ¾ cup of sauce over noodles. Top with ½ of the spinach mixture, spreading it evenly with the back of a spoon. Place another layer of lasagna noodles over spinach mixture. Spread ¾ cup of sauce atop noodles, then spread remaining spinach mixture over sauce. Add a final layer of noodles and top with remaining tomato sauce. Sprinkle Parmesan cheese over sauce.

Cook on low for 5 hours, until noodles are tender and lasagna holds together when tested with a knife.

When assembling this incredibly easy lasagna, remember this little refrain: Sauce, noodles, sauce, spinach, noodles, sauce, spinach, noodles, sauce. Leftover lasagna freezes well. Thaw and reheat in the microwave before serving.

Serves: 8–10 | 30 minutes | 5 hours

Chicken Puttanesca

A dish cooked in puttanesca style is derived from the spicy legend that it was this unique combination of bold, racy ingredients that Italian "ladies of the evening," or puttana, threw together after a long night on the street.

8 ounces dried miniature penne pasta

2 tablespoons olive oil

1½ pounds boneless, skinless chicken breasts, sliced thin

¾ cup chopped sweet onions, like Vidalia

2 teaspoons garlic paste or minced garlic

2 (14.5-ounce) cans Diced Tomatoes with Basil, Oregano, and Garlic, with juices

4 anchovies, mashed

3 tablespoons snipped fresh basil

2 tablespoons chopped kalamata olives

1 tablespoon capers, drained

⅛ teaspoon cayenne pepper

Place a large pot of water over high heat. When water has come to a full boil, add pasta, reduce heat to medium, and cook until al dente, following package instructions, about 9 minutes. Drain pasta.

While water is coming to a boil and pasta is cooking, preheat oven to 200°F. Place olive oil in a large nonstick skillet over medium-high heat. When oil is hot, add chicken slices. Sauté, stirring frequently, for 3 minutes or until chicken is just cooked through. Transfer chicken to an ovenproof dish and place it in oven to keep warm.

Return skillet to heat. Add onions and cook 1½ minutes, stirring frequently. Add garlic and cook for 30 seconds. Reduce heat to medium-low. Stir in tomatoes, anchovies, basil, olives, capers, and cayenne pepper. Cover and cook sauce 5 minutes, stirring occasionally. Return chicken to skillet. Stir to mix chicken and sauce. Cover and cook for 2 to 3 minutes more. Serve puttanesca over penne pasta.

 You do not need to salt this dish. The anchovies and unrinsed capers provide all the necessary saltiness. Kalamata olives are salty, flavorful Greek olives. You can find them in the Italian section of your supermarket.

Serves: 6 | 15 minutes | 15 minutes

Linguine with Clam Sauce

This version of the classic "spaghetti vongole" uses canned clams, rather than fresh clams in the shell. Made mostly from pantry items, this recipe, doubled, is a lifesaver when unexpected company stops by at dinnertime.

12 ounces dried linguine

1 tablespoon olive oil

1 tablespoon butter

⅓ cup chopped shallots

2 teaspoons minced garlic

1 tablespoon flour

½ cup dry white wine

1 cup bottled clam juice

1 (10-ounce) can whole baby clams, drained, juice reserved

1 cup seeded and chopped plum tomatoes

⅛ teaspoon red pepper flakes

¼ teaspoon dried basil

¼ cup snipped fresh flat-leaf parsley

Bring a large pot of water to boil over high heat. Add linguine and cook to al dente, following package instructions, about 9 minutes. Drain pasta.

While pasta is cooking, place olive oil and butter in a large nonstick skillet over medium heat. When butter has melted, add shallots and garlic and sauté, stirring constantly, for 1 minute. Stir in flour. Add wine, bottled clam juice, and reserved clam juice, and whisk until thickened, about 2 minutes. Reduce heat to low. Add clams, tomatoes, red pepper flakes, basil, and parsley. Cook sauce, stirring frequently, until clams have heated through, about 2 minutes.

Add drained linguine to clam sauce and toss so that pasta is well-coated with sauce. Serve immediately.

 Shallots keep for weeks in your refrigerator. A part of the onion family, they impart a stronger flavor than their cousins, so if you don't have them, substitute ½ cup chopped onions instead. Substitute 2 (6.5-ounce) cans minced or chopped clams for the whole baby clams if you like. Fresh parsley is important in this recipe (see Stocking the Pantry, 'Fridge, and Freezer section), but you can substitute 1 teaspoon dried parsley in a pinch. To easily seed a plum tomato, cut tomato in half and scoop out the seeds with your finger.

Serves: 3–4 | 8 minutes | 10 minutes

Spaghetti and Neapolitan-style Meatballs

The addition of pine nuts (pignolia), currants, and parsley distinguish these meatballs, which are similar to those traditionally eaten in the Campania area of Italy near Naples. Quickly baked in a mini-muffin pan, the 24 meatballs can be made ahead and frozen until needed, cutting the final prep/cook time to about 12 minutes.

1¼ pounds ground beef

1 cup panko bread crumbs

½ cup plus 2 tablespoons shredded
    Parmesan cheese

2½ tablespoons milk

3 large eggs, beaten

1 teaspoon minced garlic

½ cup currants or raisins

½ cup pine nuts

¼ cup snipped fresh flat-leaf parsley or
    2 tablespoons dried parsley

2 teaspoons salt, divided

½ teaspoon black pepper

1 (26-ounce) jar of your favorite prepared
    pasta sauce

1 (14.5-ounce) can Petite Cut Diced
    Tomatoes with Garlic and Olive Oil

2 pounds dried spaghetti or angel hair pasta

Preheat oven to 375°F. Place ground beef, bread crumbs, Parmesan cheese, milk, eggs, garlic, currants, pine nuts, parsley, 1 teaspoon salt, and pepper in a large bowl. Using clean hands, mix ingredients well.

Coat a 24-slot mini-muffin pan with vegetable cooking oil. Shape meat mixture into small balls, about 1½ inch in diameter, and place one in each mini-muffin slot. Bake for 15 minutes, until meat is just cooked through and browned on the outside.

While meatballs are cooking, place a large pot of water to boil over high heat, adding 1 teaspoon salt. In a large saucepan over medium heat, place pasta sauce and diced tomatoes. When mixture is hot, reduce heat to low. When meatballs are done, add them to sauce and heat on low for 5 minutes or until spaghetti is cooked.

Add spaghetti to boiling water and cook to al dente, following package directions, about 9 minutes. Turn off burner and drain spaghetti. Return spaghetti to pan. (Put pan on turned-off burner if meatballs and sauce have not yet heated together for 5 minutes.)

Serve spaghetti with meatballs and sauce.

 To serve 4, use only 1 pound of pasta and half the meatballs and sauce mixture. Freeze the other half for another meal. Or, use leftover meatballs and sauce to make Meatball Hoagies (page 29).

Serves: 8 (3 meatballs per serving) | 20 minutes | (*!*) 15–20 minutes

Chicken Tetrazzini

When you have a few extra weekend minutes, pay it forward and take the time to do the prep work for this warmly comforting pasta dish. Refrigerate assembled tetrazzini for a day or two or freeze it for up to a month. (The flavors are better when they marry for a while.) So when you're confronted with a particularly busy day, reap the rewards and have a glass of wine while dinner bakes itself in a mere 25 minutes.

8 ounces dried angel hair pasta

3 tablespoons butter

8 ounces mushrooms, stemmed, wiped clean, and sliced

1 tablespoon lemon juice

1 (1.25-ounce) McCormick Creamy Garlic Alfredo Sauce Mix

1 cup milk

1 cup chicken broth

2 tablespoons sherry

1 store-bought rotisserie chicken, chopped into bite-size pieces (about 4 cups)

¾ cup Parmesan cheese

Up to two days ahead: Bring a large pot of water to boil over high heat. Add angel hair pasta and cook to al dente, following package instructions, about 7 minutes. Drain and set aside until needed.

Melt butter in a large skillet over medium heat. Add mushrooms and lemon juice and sauté for 2 minutes. Remove from heat. Toss pasta with mushroom mixture and set aside.

Place a medium saucepan over medium heat. Add sauce mix, milk, broth, and sherry. Bring to a boil, stirring occasionally, then reduce heat to medium-low and cook for 2 minutes, stirring frequently.

Place chicken in a large bowl. Pour sauce over chicken and toss to coat chicken thoroughly with sauce. Coat a 9x13-inch baking dish with vegetable cooking spray. Spread angel hair–mushroom mixture in dish. Spoon chicken and sauce evenly atop the pasta. Sprinkle tetrazzini with Parmesan cheese.

To bake: Preheat oven to 400°F. Bake 20–25 minutes, uncovered, until bubbly and heated through.

 If your budget allows, substitute sautéed shrimp for the chicken for an elegant company meal. If you have cooked angel hair pasta left over from another meal, simply place it in a colander and pour hot water over it, to separate strands. If you are really pressed for time, substitute canned mushrooms, but fresh taste much better. You can omit the sherry, but it adds a special, authentic tetrazzini taste to the dish.

Serves: 6–8 | 25 minutes | 20–25 minutes

Slow Cooker Pasta Bolognese

Pure comfort food in the northern Italian region of Emilia-Romagna, this sauce is named for its capital city — Bologna. Thick and rich, the meat sauce is traditionally simmered for hours, a process that breaks down the meat and concentrates the flavors. Perfectly suited for the slow cooker, this recipe makes enough sauce to freeze for several future meals.

1½ tablespoons olive oil, divided
3 cups chopped sweet onions, like Vidalia
½ cup diced carrots
½ cup diced celery
2 teaspoons minced garlic
2 pounds ground beef (90% lean)
½ cup white wine

2 (28-ounce) cans Diced Tomatoes with Basil, Garlic, and Oregano
1 (6-ounce) can tomato paste
2 teaspoons salt
1½ teaspoon black pepper
2 pounds dried tagliatelle or fettuccine
Parmesan cheese

Heat 1 tablespoon oil in a large skillet over medium heat. Add onions, carrots, celery, and garlic. Sauté, stirring frequently, until onion is soft but not browned, about 3 minutes. Transfer vegetable mixture to slow cooker.

Add ½ tablespoon oil to skillet. Add beef and cook through, stirring frequently to break beef into small bits, about 5 minutes. Drain beef in a colander and return to skillet. Add wine and cook, stirring constantly, for 1 minute. Transfer beef and wine to slow cooker. Add tomatoes and tomato paste to slow cooker. Season with salt and pepper. Stir to combine all ingredients.

Cover slow cooker and cook on low for 6–8 hours.

To serve: Bring a large pot of water to boil over high heat. Add pasta and cook to al dente, following package instructions, about 9 minutes. Drain pasta and serve topped with Bolognese sauce. Sprinkle each serving with Parmesan cheese.

  To serve 6, use only 1 pound of pasta and half the Bolognese sauce. Freeze the other half (6 cups sauce) for another meal. The traditional pasta served with Bolognese sauce is tagliatelle, a ribbonlike pasta, slightly wider than fettuccine. In an authentic Bolognese sauce, the beef is sautéed until the wine has evaporated, then 1 cup milk is added and the beef is sautéed until the milk, too, has evaporated. You can add this step into the recipe if you have the time, but the sauce tastes great without it.

Serves: 12 | 22 minutes | 6–8 hours in slow cooker / 10 minutes for pasta

Hamburger Stroganoff

Created in the late 1800s in St. Petersburg, Russia, beef stroganoff was the brain child of Count Alexandrovich Stroganoff's master chef. Traditionally a rich concoction of beef tenderloin, mushrooms, and sour cream, stroganoff loses nothing in the translation to this quick, low-cost version.

2 tablespoons butter
1⅓ pound ground beef (85% lean)
½ cup chopped sweet onions, like Vidalia
2 teaspoons garlic paste or minced garlic
2 tablespoons flour
½ teaspoon salt
¼ teaspoon pepper

8 ounces fresh mushrooms, stems removed, wiped clean, and sliced
¼ cup Asian sweet chili sauce
½ teaspoon Worcestershire sauce
1¼ cups beef broth
8–9 ounces dried egg noodles
1 cup sour cream

Place a large pot of water over medium heat and bring to a boil.

Melt butter in a large nonstick skillet over medium heat. Add ground beef and onions and cook, stirring frequently, until beef is no longer pink, about 5 minutes. Stir in garlic, flour, salt, and pepper. Cook for 1 minute, stirring constantly. Add mushrooms, chili sauce, Worcestershire sauce, and broth. Stir to combine. Reduce heat to low and simmer, uncovered, for 10 minutes.

Meanwhile, as beef mixture is simmering, add egg noodles to boiling water. Reduce heat to medium-high. Cook noodles, uncovered, stirring occasionally, following package instructions, until al dente, about 10–12 minutes. Drain cooked noodles in a colander.

Stir sour cream into stroganoff and heat through, about 2 minutes (do not allow to boil or sauce will curdle). Serve stroganoff over egg noodles.

 You can partially prepare this recipe ahead. Simmer beef mixture for only 2 minutes, instead of 10. Cool in refrigerator and then store in a covered container until needed. Reheat beef mixture for 8 minutes over medium-low heat. Reduce heat to low, add sour cream, and heat for 2 minutes more.

Asian sweet chili sauce is available in most supermarkets in the international foods section. It adds a sweet yet spicy zing to the stroganoff, but if need be, you can substitute traditional chili sauce.

Serves: 4 | 5 minutes | 🕐 20 minutes

Spaghetti Carbonara

Legend has it that Spaghetti Carbonara originated near Rome, its name meaning "charcoal," its recipe devised by coal miners. Whatever its origins, this spaghetti is comfortingly rich with cream, butter, eggs, and Parmesan, punctuated by the smoky flavor of bacon.

6 slices bacon, cut into ½-inch pieces

½ cup chopped sweet onions, like Vidalia

1 clove garlic, minced (about 1½ teaspoons)

1 pound dried spaghetti

2 tablespoons butter

1 cup EggBeaters (with yolks)

5 tablespoons heavy cream

½ teaspoon black pepper

1 cup grated Parmesan cheese

Place a large pot of water over high heat and bring to a boil. Meanwhile, place bacon, onions, and garlic in a large nonstick skillet over medium heat. Cook, stirring occasionally, until bacon is cooked through, but not crispy, about 8 minutes. Place a strainer over a medium bowl and drain grease from bacon mixture. Return bacon mixture and 1 tablespoon bacon grease to skillet and warm over low heat.

When water comes to a boil, add pasta. Reduce heat to medium and cook spaghetti to al dente, stirring occasionally, about 9 minutes. (After 7 minutes, taste pasta each minute to assure pasta does not overcook.) Drain pasta in a colander, then toss it with butter in a large bowl.

While pasta is cooking, mix EggBeaters, heavy cream, black pepper, and ½ cup Parmesan cheese together with a wire whisk. Add this cheese mixture to hot, drained pasta and toss quickly so that pasta is well sauced, but EggBeaters do not scramble. Add bacon mixture to pasta and toss. Twirl spaghetti around a large fork and place pasta mounds on individual plates. Top with remaining Parmesan cheese and black pepper to taste.

 Authentic carbonara recipes call for raw eggs. EggBeaters with yolks provide a successful, healthful alternative. The eggs in this product are commercially pasteurized, which kills any potential salmonella. The difference in taste is negligible.

Serves: 4 | 6 minutes | 🕐 22 minutes

Penne with Fresh Tomato Sauce and Shrimp

Watch your supermarket ads for special sales of frozen shrimp and stock up. You won't need many to jazz up this super-easy fresh tomato sauce. Don't have shrimp? Don't worry. The sauce is fantastic all by itself.

¾ pound penne pasta

1½ pounds Roma tomatoes

½ pound mozzarella cheese

¾ cup snipped fresh basil

7 tablespoons olive oil, divided

2 tablespoons red wine vinegar

1 teaspoon minced garlic

1 teaspoon kosher salt

1 teaspoon cracked black pepper

12 ounces medium raw shrimp with shells

½ teaspoon McCormick Garlic Herb Seasoning Blend

6 tablespoons grated Parmesan cheese

Place a large pot of water over high heat and bring to a boil. Place penne in boiling water, reduce heat to medium, and cook pasta until al dente, about 9 minutes.

While water comes to a boil and pasta is cooking, cut Roma tomatoes in half, remove seeds, and chop into ½-inch dice. (You'll have about 3 cups chopped tomatoes.) Place in a large bowl. Cut mozzarella into ½-inch dice and place in bowl. Add basil, 6 tablespoons olive oil, vinegar, garlic, salt, and pepper to bowl, and toss to mix ingredients well. Set aside.

Peel and devein shrimp. Rinse shrimp, pat dry with paper toweling, and place in a medium bowl. Toss seasoning blend with shrimp. Place 1 tablespoon oil in a large nonstick skillet over medium heat. When oil is hot, add shrimp and sauté, stirring constantly, for 3 minutes, until shrimp are pink and just cooked through. Remove from heat.

Drain al dente pasta and place in large bowl with fresh tomato sauce. Toss to coat pasta with tomato sauce. (The warm pasta heats up the sauce and melts the cheese slightly.) Add shrimp and toss again to mix. Sprinkle each portion with 1 tablespoon Parmesan cheese.

 Pop a loaf of bake it yourself bread in the oven when you start cooking the pasta. The bread will be done when you toss the pasta together, about 9 minutes later.

Can't afford shrimp and mozzarella this month? Substitute feta cheese and spinach instead.

Serves: 6 | 17 minutes | 🕐 4 minutes

Peanut Noodles

Noodles are comfort food in many cultures. These subtly flavored, Asian-inspired peanut noodles make a great accompaniment for fish, seafood, or poultry dishes. Or, top the noodles with sautéed shrimp (see instructions in Penne with Fresh Tomato Sauce and Shrimp, page 55) for a main-course meal.

4 ounces dried linguine

3 tablespoons olive oil, divided

1 tablespoon creamy peanut butter

2 tablespoons soy sauce

1 tablespoon water

1 tablespoon sugar

½ tablespoon gingerroot paste or finely minced gingerroot

Dash of hot sauce

1 teaspoon sesame oil

⅓ cup chopped scallions

Bring a large pot of water to boil over high heat. Add linguine and cook to al dente, following package instructions, about 9 minutes. Drain pasta. Place pasta in a large mixing bowl and toss with 1 tablespoon olive oil. Set aside.

While pasta is cooking, place peanut butter, soy sauce, water, sugar, gingerroot, and hot sauce in a medium bowl. Whisk until smooth. Slowly pour in 2 tablespoons olive oil, whisking constantly until smooth.

Pour sauce over linguine and toss to combine. Drizzle sesame oil over noodles and toss again. Sprinkle noodles with scallions and toss one more time. Serve immediately or refrigerate in a covered container until needed. Serve cold, at room temperature, or microwave for 2 minutes to serve warm.

 The next time you make linguine for another recipe (see Linguine with Clam Sauce, page 49), make ½ pound extra pasta (about 2½ cups) and refrigerate it in a zipper bag for up to a week. To use leftover pasta in this recipe, place it in a colander and pour boiling water over it to heat it and separate the strands. (It is important that the noodles are cooked only to al dente.) This recipe is especially easy when you have cooked noodles on hand.

Serves: 4 | 12 minutes | 2 minutes

When Company Comes

• When the Occasion Calls
for Something Special •

Thai Salmon Cakes

Fish and Chips

Flounder Almondine

Salmon in Puff Pastry

Cheesy Crab-Mushroom Quiche

Chicken Piccata

Bruschetta Chicken

Orange-Glazed Cornish Hens

Cookout Kabobs

Gourmet Mini Meatloaves

Steak on the Grill

Blackberry-Glazed Pork Tenderloin

Slow Cooker Pulled Pork

Ham Steak with Bourbon Red-Eye Gravy

Thai Salmon Cakes

Crab cakes are a perennial favorite and comfort food to many. But good-quality crabmeat is expensive. These salmon cakes, made with canned wild Alaskan red salmon, are moist, flavorful, and fresh tasting. You may never eat crab cakes again!

2 (14.75-ounce) cans wild Alaskan red salmon, drained

1 ½ tablespoons wasabi powder

1 ½ tablespoons water

½ cup mayonnaise

1 teaspoon lemon juice

Pinch of kosher salt

¼ cup snipped fresh basil

4 teaspoons fish sauce

⅔ cup chopped scallions (about 4 scallions)

2 ½ cups panko (Japanese) bread crumbs, divided

⅓ cup sesame seeds

3 tablespoons canola oil

Remove skin from salmon and pick through to remove backbones and little round spinal bones. Flake into a large bowl. Mix wasabi powder and water in a small bowl. Stir in mayonnaise, lemon juice, and salt. Add this wasabi mayonnaise, basil, fish sauce, scallions, and I cup bread crumbs to salmon. Toss to mix ingredients well. Place remaining I ½ cups bread crumbs and the sesame seeds onto a dinner plate. Stir to mix.

Press salmon mixture into a round 3-inch-diameter cookie cutter, forming a 1-inch-deep cake. Remove cutter and place cake on bread crumbs. Gently press bread crumbs onto top, bottom, and sides of cake. Transfer to a large plate. Repeat process with remaining salmon mixture, forming 8 salmon cakes in all. (You can make salmon cakes up to this point earlier in the day and refrigerate, covered, until needed.)

Heat canola oil in a large nonstick skillet over medium heat. Add salmon cakes and cook for 2 minutes. Turn cakes with a firm spatula and cook 2–3 minutes more, until cakes are golden brown on both sides. Serve immediately.

 Serve salmon cakes atop Peanut-Raisin Rice Pilaf (page 107) or a green salad tossed with Asian dressing (see Southeast Asian Chicken Salad, page 80). Commercially prepared wasabi mayonnaise is available in most supermarkets, but it is pricey.

Serves: 4 (2 salmon cakes per serving) | 30 minutes | 5 minutes

Fish and Chips

Lightened from the traditional deep-fried standards, these pan-fried tilapia fillets and baked chili and cheese fries are enhanced by a quick, homemade tartar sauce. You can make the sauce and fry the fish while the fries are baking, all in less than 30 minutes.

1 teaspoon chili powder

Coarse salt and freshly ground black pepper

¼ teaspoon dried oregano

½ teaspoon garlic powder, divided

⅛ teaspoon ground cumin

1 tablespoon Parmesan cheese

1 (32-ounce) package frozen crinkle-cut French fried potatoes

½ cup mayonnaise

2 tablespoons finely chopped sweet pickle

½ tablespoon finely chopped scallions

½ tablespoon finely chopped pimento-stuffed olives

1 teaspoon rice vinegar

1 teaspoon lemon juice

1 egg

2 teaspoons honey

1 cup seasoned fish breading mix

¼ cup olive oil, divided

1 pound (4) tilapia fillets, or any firm, white fish fillets

For the fries: Mix chili powder, ¼ teaspoon salt, oregano, ¼ teaspoon garlic powder, and cumin in a small bowl. In another small bowl, mix Parmesan cheese, ¼ teaspoon salt, ¼ teaspoon garlic powder, and ¼ teaspoon black pepper.

Preheat oven to 450°F. Line a baking sheet with aluminum foil. Coat foil with olive oil spray. Place fries on foil and coat all sides with olive oil spray. Sprinkle chili seasoning atop half the fries, cheese seasoning atop the other half. Toss to coat fries well with seasonings, keeping the sides separate. Bake for 10 minutes. Turn fries and bake 10 minutes more.

For the tartar sauce: While fries are baking, mix mayonnaise, sweet pickle, scallions, olives, vinegar, lemon juice, and pinch of coarse salt together in a small bowl. Refrigerate until needed. (Makes ⅔ cup.)

For the fish: Whisk egg and honey together in a shallow bowl. Place breading mix on a dinner plate. Place 2 tablespoons oil in each of 2 large nonstick skillets over medium heat. Dip both sides of each fish fillet in egg mixture and then coat both sides with breading. Place in skillet and cook for 2 minutes. Turn fillets with a firm spatula. Cook for 1–2 minutes longer, until fish is golden and flakes with a fork. Serve fried fish with tartar sauce, chili fries, and cheese fries.

 You can make tartar sauce ahead and refrigerate it for up to 1 week.

Serves: 4 | 🍽 Fish: 6½ minutes; Fries: 9½ minutes; Tartar sauce: 7 minutes |
⏱ Fish: 4–5 minutes; Fries: 20 minutes

Flounder Almondine

Rich and buttery, this easy fish recipe evokes memories of dining seaside in the summer or being on winter break in the Caribbean islands. With the advent of flash-frozen fish fillets, you can re-create the experience any time of the year for a fraction of the cost.

1 (16-ounce) package frozen flounder fillets, defrosted, rinsed, and dried

Salt and black pepper

1 tablespoon plus 2 teaspoons lemon juice

½ cup flour

6 tablespoons butter

½ cup slivered almonds

1 tablespoon snipped fresh parsley

3 tablespoons canola oil

Season flounder fillets with salt and pepper to taste and sprinkle them with 2 teaspoons lemon juice. Place flour on a dinner plate. Press both sides of fillets into flour until well coated. Set aside on a separate dinner plate.

Melt butter in a medium nonstick skillet over medium-low heat. Add almonds and sauté, stirring constantly, until they are lightly browned, about 2 minutes. Remove skillet from heat. Add 1 tablespoon lemon juice and stir constantly as it foams up. Stir in parsley. Set aside until needed.

Heat oil in a large nonstick skillet over medium heat. Add flounder fillets and sauté for 3 minutes, until lightly browned on the undersides. Gently turn fillets with a firm spatula. Sauté 2 minutes more, until undersides of fillets are golden and fish flakes when tested with a fork. Transfer fillets to a serving platter.

Reheat almond-butter mixture over low heat for about 1 minute. Spoon mixture over flounder fillets and serve immediately.

You can use any white-fleshed fish fillets in this recipe. Flounder fillets are thin. Adjust cooking time of thicker fillets accordingly.

Serves: 3 | 5 minutes | Sauce: 7 minutes; Fish: 5 minutes

Salmon in Puff Pastry

Call it salmon en croute, and your party guests will think they are eating in a French restaurant. This special occasion dish requires a mere 30 minutes prep time, but looks and tastes like a chef-prepared creation. When serving a large group, the cost per person can't be beat.

1 (17.3-ounce) package puff pastry
  (2 sheets)
1 (2½- to 3-pound) skinless salmon fillet
½ teaspoon salt
½ teaspoon black pepper

2 (5.2-ounce) packages Boursin garlic
  and herb cheese spread
1 (9-ounce) package fresh baby spinach,
  chopped (about 4 packed cups)
1 egg, beaten with 2 tablespoons water

Early in the day: Place one sheet of puff pastry on a floured surface. Using a rolling pin, roll pastry to form an 18x10-inch rectangle. Transfer rolled pastry to a baking sheet. Place salmon atop pastry. (Make sure you have about ¾-inch pastry surrounding salmon on all sides.) Sprinkle with salt and pepper.

Spread cheese over top and sides of salmon. Top with chopped spinach, pressing spinach into cheese and mounding excess on top. Brush egg wash on pastry surrounding salmon.

Roll remaining sheet of pastry to same size as the first. Place on top of salmon, draping it around salmon and atop bottom pastry sheet. Cut any excess from bottom layer of pastry and reserve. Press pastry edges together and roll to form a sealed border around salmon. Brush pastry with egg wash. (Roll out pastry scraps, if desired, and cut into decorative shapes with small cookie cutters. Place on top of encased salmon and brush with egg wash.)

Cover pastry-encased salmon with plastic wrap and aluminum foil and refrigerate until needed.

To bake: Preheat oven to 400°F. Bring salmon to room temperature (about 30 minutes before baking). Bake for 30 minutes, until pastry is golden. Transfer salmon to a large serving platter. Cut into 1½-inch-wide slices, then cut each slice in half.

 You can allow this dish to cool after baking and then refrigerate it until needed. Serve at room temperature. You also have the option to assemble this dish ahead of time and freeze it until needed. Place frozen salmon on a baking sheet and bake for 50–60 minutes, until golden and cooked through. You can freeze leftover baked salmon and defrost and serve it cold or at room temperature. For a small group, use individual salmon fillets and follow procedure above, using puff pastry sheets cut to size.

Serves: 16–20 | 30 minutes | 🕐 30 minutes

Cheesy Crab-Mushroom Quiche

My guests have declared this recipe "sinfully, decadently delicious." And truth be told, who doesn't willingly welcome a few extra calories when longing for a Brie fix?

⅓ cup fresh bread crumbs

1 cup sliced button mushrooms

3 scallions, white and green parts chopped

4 ounces imitation crabmeat, roughly chopped

½ cup shredded 6 Cheese Italian cheese

⅓ cup grated Parmesan cheese

8 ounces Brie cheese, rind removed and thinly sliced

3 eggs

1 cup heavy cream

½ cup whole milk

¼ cup flour

½ teaspoon kosher salt (or ⅛ teaspoon Old Bay Seasoning)

⅛ teaspoon white pepper

Early in the day or the day before: Coat a deep-dish pie plate with vegetable cooking spray. Sprinkle bread crumbs in the bottom. Spread mushrooms in pie plate and top with scallions. Place crabmeat evenly over vegetables. Sprinkle shredded cheese, then Parmesan cheese over crabmeat. Place slices of Brie in a double circle like spokes in a wheel. Cover with plastic wrap and refrigerate until needed.

Whisk eggs, cream, and milk together in a medium bowl. Whisk in flour and salt (or seasoning). Cover with plastic wrap and refrigerate until needed.

To bake: Preheat oven to 350°F. Whisk egg mixture and pour into pie plate. Bake uncovered for 30–35 minutes, until custard sets up. Serve immediately.

 Commonly marketed as "crab-flavored seafood," imitation crabmeat is actually a white fish called pollock. It is about one-quarter the cost of fresh crabmeat, and in a dish such as this, makes a cost-effective substitution for the real thing. You'll usually find this pretender near the fresh seafood section of your supermarket in 8-ounce packages. Freeze the unused portion for the next time you make this quiche.

Serves: 6 | 19 minutes | 🕐 30 minutes

Chicken Piccata

You also can use this recipe to make Veal Piccata or Fish Piccata. Simply reduce your cooking time based on the thickness of the meat or fish.

6 (4-ounce) boneless, skinless chicken breasts (about 1½ pounds)
Salt and black pepper
6 tablespoons butter, divided
¼ cup canola oil
½ cup white wine
¼ cup lemon juice
¼ cup capers, rinsed and drained
½ cup snipped fresh parsley or 2 tablespoons dried
¾ cup coarsely chopped canned artichoke hearts

Take a quart-size, freezer-weight zipper bag, and using kitchen scissors, cut off the zipper end and cut down each of the 2 perpendicular sides. Place one chicken breast at a time between the layers of the bag and pound chicken to ¼-inch thickness with a mallet. Season with salt and pepper and set aside.

Melt 2 tablespoons butter in a large nonstick skillet over medium heat. Add the oil and swirl to combine. Add chicken breasts and sauté, 1 minute per side. Transfer chicken to a platter and cover with aluminum foil. Pour off oil mixture.

Melt remaining 4 tablespoons butter in the skillet. Add wine and lemon juice and bring to a boil. Stir in capers, parsley, and artichoke hearts. Reduce heat to medium-low. Add chicken breasts to skillet. Spoon piccata sauce over chicken and simmer for 3 minutes. Turn chicken and simmer 3 minutes more or until just cooked through when tested with a knife. To serve, place chicken breasts on 4 individual plates. Spoon sauce over chicken.

 Fresh lemon juice is a key ingredient in this recipe. See Time- and Money-Saving Tips (page 133) for squeeze-and-freeze ideas.

Serves: 6 | 10 minutes | 🕐 15 minutes

Bruschetta Chicken

You may not recognize this as comfort food . . . yet . . . but you will as soon as you taste the flavorful bruschetta topping. This dish is fast, easy, and showy enough for company.

2½ cups chopped, seeded plum tomatoes
¼ cup capers, rinsed and drained
⅓ cup minced shallots
1 cup chopped onions
¼ cup snipped fresh basil
⅓ cup fresh lemon juice
1 teaspoon salt
½ teaspoon black pepper
¼ cup plus 2 tablespoons olive oil
4 boneless, skinless chicken breasts

Mix together tomatoes, capers, shallots, onions, basil, lemon juice, salt, pepper, and ¼ cup olive oil in a medium bowl. Transfer to a covered container and refrigerate until needed.

Preheat broiler. Place 2 tablespoons olive oil in a large nonstick skillet over medium heat. Brown chicken on both sides, about 2 minutes per side. Place chicken breasts on a slotted broiler pan. Top the breasts with equal amounts of tomato mixture. (Use all the tomato mixture, making a large mound over each breast; the mixture will reduce as it cooks.)

Make sure broiler pan is 4 inches from heating element. Broil chicken breasts for 15 minutes, until just barely pink when cut with a knife. (Chicken will continue cooking after it is removed from oven.) Remove chicken from oven and serve immediately, topped with bruschetta mixture.

 You can make the tomato topping up to 2 days ahead and refrigerate in a covered container. Shallots are essential to this recipe. You'll find them near the onions in your supermarket. Be careful when you remove broiler pan from oven. The lower pan will be filled with excess liquid from the bruschetta topping.

Serves: 4 | 15 minutes | 🕐 19 minutes

Orange-Glazed Cornish Hens

Elegant, economical, and easy, these glazed hens will earn you well-deserved applause at your next special dinner for family or friends. You can make the glaze days in advance, so you can bake this creation in less than 30 minutes.

2 tablespoons raspberry honey mustard or other fruit-flavored honey mustard

1 tablespoon grated orange peel

½ cup orange juice

¼ cup honey

⅛ teaspoon ground nutmeg

Cracked black pepper

Kosher or coarse salt

½ cup Triple Sec

2 teaspoons cornstarch

1 tablespoon water

2 (each 1¼- to 1½-pound) Cornish hens

To make the glaze: Place mustard, orange peel, orange juice, honey, nutmeg, 1 teaspoon pepper, and 1 teaspoon salt in a small saucepan over medium heat. Stir to combine. When honey and mustard have melted and mixture is smooth, stir in Triple Sec. Combine cornstarch and water in a small cup. Add to orange juice mixture and stir to combine. Reduce heat to medium-low and cook glaze, stirring constantly, until thickened, about 3 minutes. Remove from heat. (You can refrigerate glaze in a covered container for up to 1 week. Bring to room temperature before using.)

Preheat oven to 475°F. Cut each Cornish hen in half through the breastbone and backbone. Cut out the backbone from each hen. Wash and dry hens. Season hens with salt and pepper. Line a baking sheet with aluminum foil. Coat foil with vegetable cooking spray. Place hen halves on foil, breast side up. Coat hens with olive oil spray.

Drizzle several teaspoonfuls of glaze over each hen half, coating them well. Bake for 10 minutes. Repeat glazing process and bake for 10 minutes more. Glaze hens one more time and return them to oven for 5–10 more minutes, until tender. (Glaze will burn onto the foil but will not burn on the hens.) Remove hens and place on individual dinner plates. Serve on a bed of Peanut Noodles (page 56) along with Steamed Carrots tossed with Sesame-Orange Sauce (page 90).

 You can substitute Cointreau or Grand Marnier for the Triple Sec, or eliminate it entirely and use ½ cup more orange juice instead. Look for fruit-flavored mustard that has whole mustard seeds in the mixture. It adds a special zing to the flavor.

Serves: 4 | 26 minutes | 25–30 minutes

Cookout Kabobs

For people of the Middle East, Africa, Central and South Asia, as well as countries bordering the Mediterranean Sea, kabobs constitute pure comfort food. Consisting of grilled or broiled meats on a skewer or stick, kabobs have made their way around the world and rank high on the must-eat-at-a-summer-cookout for folks in America as well.

YOGURT-ONION CHICKEN KABOBS

The blanketing pita breads keep the chicken warm. The breads underneath the chicken absorb extra juices and are very tasty. Rip off portions of the bread and eat them with the kabobs.

2½ pounds skinless, boneless chicken breasts	¼ teaspoon black pepper
1 medium sweet onion, like Vidalia	½ tablespoon fresh lemon juice
1½ cups plain yogurt	6 plum tomatoes
1 teaspoon salt	1 package pita breads

Up to 48 hours ahead: Trim all visible fat from chicken breasts. Cut chicken breasts into 1-inch cubes. Place chicken in a large nonmetal container. Grate onion in a food processor. Add grated onions and their juices to the chicken cubes. Mix well. Add yogurt, salt, and pepper and mix well. Add lemon juice. Mix well, making sure every piece is covered with the yogurt marinade.

Cover container and marinate at least overnight. (After 24 hours of marinating, chicken-yogurt mixture can be frozen for future use.)

To cook: Preheat grill to medium-high heat. Thread chicken on metal skewers so that cubes will lie flat on the grill. Thread plum tomatoes on separate skewers. Grill chicken kabobs 10 minutes, turning twice, until chicken is just cooked through and still juicy. (Do not overcook. Chicken will continue cooking after it is removed from the grill.) Place tomato skewers on grill for the final minute the chicken is cooking.

To serve: Place one layer of pita breads on a serving tray. Remove cooked chicken from skewers and place over the bread. Top chicken with a blanket of pita bread. Remove tomatoes from skewers and place around perimeter of the serving platter.

 For both chicken and sirloin kabobs, use metal skewers whose shafts are flat, not round. That way, the meat pieces stay securely on the skewers and don't rotate around. If using wooden skewers, soak them in water for 30 minutes before threading. This will keep them from burning on the grill.

Serves: 6 | 15 minutes | Advance marinating time: 24–48 hours | 🕐 10 minutes

66

GRILLED SIRLOIN KABOBS

The longer these colorful kabobs marinate, the better they are. You can start marinating the steak up to 48 hours ahead.

3 pounds sirloin steak, cut 1½ inches thick
1 (24-ounce) bottle Zesty Italian salad dressing
1 yellow bell pepper
1 red bell pepper
1 large sweet onion, like Vidalia

Up to 48 hours ahead: Cut sirloin steak into 2-inch chunks. Place meat in a freezer-weight zipper bag. Pour all but 1 cup salad dressing into bag. Zipper bag securely and shake bag to coat all sides of meat with dressing. Place bag inside another zipper bag, close bag, and refrigerate until needed.

Cut bell peppers into 1½-inch pieces. Cut peeled onion into quarters and separate the layers. Place peppers and onions in a zipper bag and refrigerate. About 12 hours before cooking, pour remaining 1 cup salad dressing over vegetables, reseal bag, and refrigerate until needed.

To cook: Preheat grill to medium-high heat. Thread steak, peppers, and onions alternately onto long metal skewers. Place skewers on rack of hot grill. Baste with dressing marinade. Grill skewers for 7 minutes, turning skewers 3 or 4 times. Steak will be medium-rare.

To serve: Serve the kabobs on the skewers or remove meat and vegetables and present them in a tumble on a large serving platter.

 You'll find terrific prices on sirloin steak at a price club, like Sam's, BJ's or Costco. Ask the butcher to cut the meat 1½ inches thick. He won't charge you any more for the service.

Serves: 6 | 20 minutes | Advance marinating time: 24–48 hours | 🕐 7 minutes

Gourmet Mini Meatloaves

These individual meatloaves bake in half the time of a conventional loaf. By baking them on a broiler pan, the meaty grayish juice that oozes out as they cook drips through the slots in the pan, allowing the meatloaves to brown on all sides.

2 teaspoons olive oil

1⅓ cups chopped sweet onions, like Vidalia

2 teaspoons minced garlic

2 pounds ground beef or meatloaf mix
    (beef, pork, veal)

2 cups fresh bread crumbs

2 eggs, beaten

¼ cup snipped fresh flat-leaf parsley or
    2 tablespoons dried

2 tablespoons Worcestershire sauce

½ teaspoon hot sauce

½ teaspoon dry mustard

2 teaspoons salt

½ teaspoon black pepper

½ cup ketchup

½ cup sugar

Early in the day or the day before: Heat olive oil in a medium nonstick skillet over medium heat. Add onions and garlic. Sauté for 1½ minutes. Remove from heat. Place in a large mixing bowl.

Add ground beef, bread crumbs, and eggs. With clean hands mix until ingredients are well combined. Add parsley, Worcestershire sauce, hot sauce, dry mustard, salt, and pepper. Mix seasonings into meat mixture.

Firmly pack meatloaf mixture into a 1-cup measure, mounding top to form a dome. Slide a paring knife gently around the edges of the cup. Upend cup onto your hand so that meatloaf slides out. Then place loaf, flat side down, on a tray. Repeat with remaining mixture. (You can refrigerate meatloaves, covered, at this point for up to 24 hours or freeze until needed. Bring meatloaves to room temperature before baking.)

To bake: Preheat oven to 400°F. Transfer meatloaves to the slotted tray of a broiler pan. Bake for 15 minutes. Meanwhile, place ketchup and sugar in a small saucepan over medium-low heat. Cook for 1 minute, stirring constantly, until sugar is dissolved. Spoon ketchup mixture over partially baked meatloaves. Bake meatloaves for 15 minutes more or until meat, when tested with a knife, is cooked through (155°F on instant-read thermometer).

 These 1-cup meatloaves are hearty portions. If you have a ¾-cup measure, the mixture will form 6 mini-loaves, suitable for smaller appetites.

Serves: 5 (1 mini-loaf per serving) | 20 minutes | 🕐 30 minutes

Steak on the Grill

Nothing is more comforting on a warm summer night than a thick, juicy steak on the grill. Marinate this sirloin overnight and serve with mushrooms and onions. (See Sautéed 'Shrooms and Caramelized Onions recipes, pages 93 and 94.) You won't need to serve filet mignon for your family or guests to think they are eating at a fancy steakhouse.

⅔ cup beer
⅓ cup olive oil
1 teaspoon salt
¼ teaspoon garlic powder
¼ teaspoon black pepper
2½ pounds top sirloin steak, cut 1½ inches thick

The day before: Whisk beer, oil, salt, garlic powder, and pepper together in a medium bowl. Place steak in a large freezer-weight zipper bag. Pour marinade over steak in bag. Zip bag. Place bag inside another zipper bag and close. Shake bag so that marinade evenly coats steak. Refrigerate overnight.

To cook: Preheat grill. Remove bag of marinating steak from refrigerator and let it reach room temperature. Remove steak from marinade and place it on hot grill. Cook for 5–6 minutes. Turn steak and grill for 5–6 more minutes, until steak is medium-rare. Cut steak into ½-inch slices and serve immediately with sautéed mushrooms and caramelized onions.

 Use a good ale for the marinade for best results. The marinade is equally good with grilled chicken.

Serves: 6 | 5 minutes | Marinating time: 24 hours | 10–12 minutes

Blackberry-Glazed Pork Tenderloin

Roast tenderloins to an internal temperature of 150°F for medium (warm, pink center), which is above the 137°F necessary to kill any trichinae. Be careful not to overcook pork tenderloin, one of the leanest meats you can eat. Tenderloins are more expensive than other cuts, but they cut like butter and melt in your mouth.

½ cup blackberry preserves

3 tablespoons water

2 tablespoons Worcestershire sauce

2 tablespoons cider vinegar

1 tablespoon Asian sweet chili sauce

1 (2½-pound) package pork tenderloins

2 large cloves garlic, sliced lengthwise

2 tablespoons olive oil, divided

1 teaspoon fresh rosemary

½ teaspoon kosher salt

¼ teaspoon cracked pepper

½ pint fresh blackberries (optional)

Preheat oven to 425°F. Place preserves, water, Worcestershire sauce, vinegar, and chili sauce in a small saucepan over medium heat. Cook sauce, stirring occasionally, until preserves are melted, about 2 minutes. Remove from heat and cover.

Make 4 slits in the tenderloins, several inches apart. Place garlic slices in slits. Brush top of tenderloins with 1 tablespoon oil. Sprinkle rosemary over tenderloins. Season with salt and pepper.

Heat remaining 1 tablespoon oil in a large skillet over medium-high heat. Sear the tenderloins until browned on all sides, about 3 minutes in total. Remove tenderloins from skillet and place in a foil-lined baking pan. Baste with blackberry sauce.

Place tenderloins in oven for 8 minutes. Baste with sauce and return to oven for 7 more minutes. Remove tenderloins from oven and tent with aluminum foil. Allow tenderloins to rest for 5 minutes. Cut into ½-inch slices on the diagonal. Arrange slices on a serving platter. Drizzle with blackberry sauce. Sprinkle tenderloin with blackberries if desired. Serve with remaining sauce.

 Look for supermarket sales of pork tenderloins and stock up. You can freeze them for up to 6 months. You'll find sweet chili sauce in the Asian section of your supermarket.

You can prepare blackberry sauce a day ahead and reheat before using. To save further time, you can prepare the tenderloin with garlic, oil, and rosemary early in the day, then cover and refrigerate until needed.

Serves: 6 | 15 minutes | 🕐 15 minutes | Rest time: 5 minutes

Slow Cooker Pulled Pork

Pulled pork or barbecue, as it is known in some parts, has become a competitive art form to many. Every region of the country has its own variations and customs, but the one thing they all agree on is that the pork must cook a good long time. This adaptation takes the fuss out of preparation for any busy barbecue lover.

1 tablespoon olive oil	1 teaspoon crushed red pepper flakes
1 (3½- to 4-pound) boneless pork loin	1 tablespoon Worcestershire sauce
1 cup chopped sweet onions, like Vidalia	1 teaspoon dry mustard
1 cup cider vinegar	1 teaspoon salt
¾ cup ketchup	1 teaspoon black pepper
½ cup dark molasses	Sandwich buns
½ cup dark brown sugar, packed	

Place olive oil in a large nonstick skillet over medium heat. Add pork loin and brown on all sides, about 3 minutes. Transfer to slow cooker.

Pour off remaining olive oil from pan. Add onions and sauté, stirring occasionally, until golden, about 2 minutes. Reduce heat to low. Add vinegar, ketchup, molasses, brown sugar, red pepper flakes, Worcestershire sauce, dry mustard, salt, and pepper. Stir to mix well. Increase heat to medium-high. Bring mixture to a boil and cook, stirring constantly, for I minute. Pour vinegar mixture over pork loin in slow cooker.

Cook pork on low for 10 hours or on high for 5 hours, until pork is fork-tender.

Transfer pork to cutting board and shred. Return shredded pork to sauce and stir to combine. Serve on sandwich buns. (Or, you can keep pork warm in cooker on low to serve later.)

 Typically pork shoulder or butt is used in making traditional pulled pork. But when cooked in a slow cooker instead of an oven or grill, the fat from the pork makes the sauce too greasy. The leaner cut of pork loin works better here. Although loin is a bit more expensive than shoulder or butt, you can find good sales on whole loins at price clubs and occasionally at supermarkets. Get a whole loin, cut it in pieces, and freeze for multiple uses. Freeze leftover pulled pork in sauce and reheat in microwave for a future meal.

Serves: 12 | 21 minutes | 5–10 hours

Ham Steak with Bourbon Red-Eye Gravy

The origin of the name "red-eye gravy" has as many interpretations as the recipe itself. The fact is, "red-eye" was a term used by American pioneers when referring to the watered-down whiskey often served in the era's saloons. But I think the round bone in the ham steak is the eye in question. As the ham simmers in the bourbon gravy, the marrow in the center of the bone takes on a distinctive reddish hue, looking very much like a red eye. Whatever the explanation, this dish is fantastic.

3 tablespoons dark brown sugar

3 tablespoons frozen apple juice concentrate, thawed

1 teaspoon Dijon mustard

¼ cup Jim Beam bourbon whiskey

1 teaspoon canola oil

1 (1¼-pound) ½-inch-thick ham steak

Place brown sugar, apple juice concentrate, mustard, and bourbon in a small bowl. Stir to mix until sugar has dissolved, about 1 minute.

Place oil in a large nonstick skillet over medium heat. Place ham steak in skillet and cook for 2 minutes on each side. Reduce heat to low. Add bourbon mixture and simmer for 8 minutes, turning steak about every 1½ minutes.

Cut ham into 3 servings and place on individual dinner plates. Top with bourbon red-eye gravy and serve immediately.

 Ham and red-eye gravy is a Southern classic often served for breakfast with buttered grits. The breakfast gravy is made with butter, brewed coffee, and water. Some theorize that "red eye" refers to how one feels the morning after a night on the town, a condition cured by a good jolt of coffee.

Serves: 3 | 5 minutes | 🕐 12 minutes

One-Dish Dinners

• Salads, Savory Pies, and Stir-Fries •

Orange Shrimp Stir-fry over Jasmine Rice

Stir-fry Your Way

Chicken Pot Pies

Cottage Pies

Chicken Enchiladas

Parmesan Risotto with Ham, Baby Spinach,
and Slivered Tomatoes

Southeast Asian Chicken Salad

Shrimp Waldorf Salad

Baked Nachos

Orange Shrimp Stir-fry over Jasmine Rice

Slightly spicy, slightly sweet, and faintly orangey, this stir-fry touches all your taste buds. For a more economical dish, substitute 12 ounces boneless chicken breast for the shrimp.

1 cup jasmine rice
1 pound (16–20 count) shrimp
2 tablespoons sesame seeds
¼ cup orange juice
2 tablespoons sherry
2 tablespoons rice vinegar
1 tablespoon orange marmalade
1 tablespoon Asian sweet chili sauce

1 tablespoon honey
1 tablespoon cornstarch
¼ cup canola oil, divided
1 tablespoon garlic paste or minced garlic
1 tablespoon gingerroot paste or minced gingerroot
4 cups frozen Asian mixed vegetables, cut into uniform bite-size pieces

Place 1½ cups water in a medium saucepan over high heat. When water comes to a boil, stir in rice. Reduce heat to low, place 2 pieces of paper toweling over pan, place cover on saucepan, and simmer for 15 minutes, until water is absorbed. Fluff rice with a fork before serving.

While rice is cooking, peel and devein shrimp. Place sesame seeds in a small nonstick skillet over low heat. Toast, stirring frequently, for about 1 minute. Remove from heat and set aside.

Whisk together orange juice, sherry, vinegar, marmalade, chili sauce, honey, and cornstarch in a medium bowl. Add shrimp and stir until shrimp are coated with sauce.

Heat 2 tablespoons oil in a large wok or stir-fry pan over high heat. With a slotted spoon, transfer shrimp from sauce to a plate. Add shrimp to hot oil, stirring constantly, until shrimp is pink and nearly cooked through, 1½–2 minutes. Remove shrimp to a plate and set aside until needed.

Add 1 tablespoon oil to wok. Add garlic and gingerroot and cook, stirring constantly, for 15 seconds. Add remaining tablespoon oil and frozen vegetables to wok and stir-fry, stirring constantly for 2 minutes. Stir in orange sauce and cook for 1 minute more, until sauce begins to thicken. Add shrimp and toss with vegetables. Cook for 1 minute, stirring constantly, until shrimp is heated through and coated with sauce.

Serve immediately over jasmine rice. Sprinkle each serving with toasted sesame seeds.

 The keys to a great stir-fry are to have all your ingredients prepped and ready before you start and to cook over high heat, stirring constantly.

Serves: 4 | 16 minutes | 13 minutes

Stir-fry Your Way

A good stir-fry is made up of five components: meat/seafood, marinade/sauce, aromatics, vegetables, and garnish. Mix and match ingredients from the choices below to design your own stir-fry creation. Follow the stir-fry technique described in the recipe on page 74, and serve stir-fry over steamed short- or medium-grain rice, Chinese egg noodles, or Thai rice noodles. Figure 3 ounces meat/4 ounces seafood, 1 cup vegetables, and 1 cup cooked rice per person (1 cup uncooked rice equals 3 cups cooked).

MEAT/SEAFOOD

Cut 12 ounces flank steak, pork tenderloin, or boneless chicken breasts into ¼-inch slices across grain, then into ½-inch strips lengthwise. When using seafood, increase amount to 1 pound and leave shrimp or scallops whole. Cook meat or chicken in batches so as not to crowd the pieces in the wok.

MARINADE/SAUCE

The marinade/sauce is made up of liquid, flavorings, sweetener, and cornstarch. Whisk together a total of ½ cup liquid (sherry, citrus juice, rice or white wine, broth) with a total of 2 tablespoons flavorings (chili sauce with garlic, Asian sweet chili sauce, soy sauce, hoisin sauce, oyster sauce, citrus peel, peanut butter, fish sauce, toasted sesame oil); 1 tablespoon sweetener (honey, white sugar, brown sugar); and 1 tablespoon cornstarch.

AROMATICS

1 tablespoon garlic paste or finely minced garlic and 1 tablespoon gingerroot paste or finely minced gingerroot.

VEGETABLES

Use 4 cups of bite-size vegetables — frozen or fresh. Frozen Asian vegetable medley (available in supermarket or price club frozen food sections) is usually already cut into bite-size pieces and cooks uniformly in about 3 minutes. Fresh vegetables fall into three categories of cooking times: slow, medium, and fast. Add slow-cooking vegetables first, cooking for about 3–4 minutes. Then add medium-cooking vegetables and cook about 2–3 minutes. Add fast-cooking vegetables at the very end of the stir-fry and cook for only about 30 seconds.

Slow-cooking vegetables include: asparagus, broccoli, carrots, green beans, onions, winter squash. Medium-cooking vegetables: bell peppers, celery, mushrooms, zucchini and summer squash. Fast-cooking vegetables: bean sprouts, cabbage, pea pods, scallions, spinach, tomatoes.

GARNISHES

Add garnishes to taste: freshly chopped parsley, chopped toasted nuts, toasted sesame seeds.

Serves: 4

Chicken Pot Pies

"Four and twenty blackbirds" are not baked in this pie, but chicken pot pie is thought to date back as far as the Middle Ages, when it was called a savory tart. Chefs in the royal kitchens of England and France considered the dish one of their most elaborate. This one is showy, too, but easy!

1 (15-ounce) jar small, whole, cooked onions
1 cup baby carrots, quartered lengthwise
6 tablespoons butter
6 tablespoons flour
2 cups College Inn Rotisserie Chicken Bold Stock
½ cup heavy cream
½ cup half-and-half
½ teaspoon black pepper
¼ teaspoon salt
1 teaspoon dried marjoram
1 delicatessen rotisserie chicken, cut in bite-size pieces (about 4 cups)
1 cup chopped celery
1 cup sliced fresh button mushrooms
¾ cup frozen peas, thawed
1 (10-ounce) package frozen puff pastry shells

Early in the day or the day before: Drain onions and cut them in half. Set aside. Place carrots in a microwave-proof dish and microwave for 1 minute. Set aside.

Melt butter in a large saucepan over medium-low heat. Stir in flour, 1 tablespoon at a time. Stirring constantly, slowly add stock, cream, and half-and-half. Season the cream mixture with pepper, salt, and marjoram. Cook mixture, stirring constantly, until it is slightly thickened, about 1 minute.

Add chicken, celery, mushrooms, peas, onions, and carrots. Toss ingredients until well coated with sauce. Evenly divide chicken and vegetable mixture among six 1½-cup round ramekins. Cover with plastic wrap and refrigerate until needed.

To bake: Preheat oven to 400°F. Bring pot pies to room temperature. Place frozen puff pastry shells on a nonstick baking sheet. Place pot pies and pastry shells in oven and bake for 20 minutes, until mixture is bubbly and pastry is golden.

To serve: With a tablespoon, make a well in the middle of each pot pie. Place a pastry shell in each well. Serve immediately.

 You can freeze pot pies after the initial prep stage (before adding the puff pastry). Thaw as many pot pies as you need and bring them to room temperature. Bake pot pies and puff pastry as instructed above.

Serves: 6 | 31 minutes | 🕐 20 minutes

Cottage Pies

This traditional English minced pie is called cottage pie when it is made with beef and shepherd's pie when it is made with lamb.

1 tablespoon olive oil
1½ cups chopped sweet onions, like Vidalia
½ cup chopped baby carrots
1 teaspoon garlic paste or finely minced garlic
1½ cups sliced button mushrooms
¼ teaspoon crushed red pepper flakes
¼ teaspoon dried thyme
½ teaspoon salt
1½ pounds ground beef
2 tablespoons flour
1 cup beef broth
1 (4-ounce) package Idahoan Four Cheese Mashed Potatoes mix
Salt and freshly ground black pepper

Early in the day or day before: Place oil in a large nonstick skillet over medium heat. Add onions, carrots, and garlic, and sauté, stirring frequently, for 2 minutes. Add mushrooms, red pepper flakes, thyme, and salt, and sauté for 1 minute. Set aside.

Place ground beef in a medium nonstick skillet over medium heat. Cook beef, stirring occasionally, until it is no longer pink. Drain meat in a colander and transfer to skillet with vegetable mixture. Stir to combine.

Place skillet over medium heat. Stir in flour. Slowly stir in beef broth and cook, stirring occasionally, for 2 minutes, until thickened slightly. Divide beef mixture evenly among 4 (1½-cup) ramekins. Cover with plastic wrap and aluminum foil and refrigerate or freeze until needed.

To bake: Preheat oven to 375°F. Bring cottage pies to room temperature. Place 2 cups boiling water in serving bowl. Add mashed potato mix all at once and stir with a fork to moisten. Season potatoes with salt and pepper to taste. Allow potatoes to rest for 1 minute. Top cottage pies with equal amounts of potatoes. Bake for 15 minutes, until potatoes are golden and pies are bubbly.

 Add ½ cup shredded sharp cheddar cheese for an even cheesier potato topping. You can use any leftover mashed potatoes for this recipe.

Serves: 4 | 30 minutes | 15 minutes

Chicken Enchiladas

Many supermarkets run specials on their rotisserie chickens on certain days of the week. Check listings and take advantage of the sales. You can chop up the chickens and freeze the meat for future use.

3 cups chopped rotisserie chicken or leftover cooked chicken

1 (14-ounce) can enchilada sauce, divided

1 cup chopped sweet onions, like Vidalia

1 (8-ounce) package (or 2 cups) shredded Mexican-style or taco-style cheese, divided

5 burrito-size flour tortillas

1 tomato

1 wedge iceberg lettuce

1 cup sour cream

Preheat oven to 375°F. Coat a 7x11-inch baking dish with vegetable cooking spray.

Place chicken, ¾ cup enchilada sauce, onions, and 1 cup cheese in a large bowl. Toss to mix well.

Microwave 3 tortillas for 20 seconds. Spoon ½ cup chicken mixture onto the lower third of each tortilla. Fold in the sides of each tortilla, then roll the lower edge over the filling mixture. Keep rolling, tucking in the right and left sides, until you have a large cigar-shaped roll. Place each rolled tortilla in baking dish. Microwave the remaining 2 tortillas and repeat process with the remaining chicken mixture.

Pour remaining enchilada sauce over rolled tortillas. Sprinkle remaining 1 cup cheese over the sauce. Bake for 15–20 minutes, until the cheese is melted and browned slightly.

While enchiladas are baking, chop tomato and lettuce.

To serve: Place 1 enchilada on each individual dinner plate. Sprinkle tomatoes, lettuce, and remaining shredded cheese atop enchiladas. Top with a dollop of sour cream.

 You can substitute 1 pound cooked ground beef or ground turkey for the chicken in this recipe. If you like your enchiladas extra-spicy, add a few drops of hot sauce to the enchilada sauce before baking. You can freeze the enchiladas after the prep phase. Thaw and bring to room temperature before baking.

Serves: 5 | 17 minutes | 🕑 15–20 minutes

Parmesan Risotto with Ham, Baby Spinach, and Slivered Tomatoes

A basic risotto has five components: broth (chicken, vegetable, beef, seafood), aromatics (onions, garlic, shallots, celery, carrots), fat (butter, oil, bacon fat), Arborio rice, and enhancements (cheese, seafood, vegetables, meats). Follow the simple technique described in this recipe and create a new risotto every time, just by varying ingredients. Risotto takes just 20 minutes, from the first addition of broth to the finish.

1 (48-ounce) carton low-sodium chicken broth	½ cup grated Parmesan cheese
4 tablespoons (½ stick) butter, divided	½ cup thin-sliced delicatessen honey ham,
1 cup finely chopped sweet onions,	cut into ¼-inch-wide strips
like Vidalia	3 cups chopped baby spinach
1 teaspoon garlic paste or minced garlic	1 cup quartered grape tomatoes
2 cups Arborio rice	2 tablespoons snipped fresh flat-leaf parsley
½ cup white wine	

Bring broth to simmer in a medium saucepan over medium-low heat. Reduce heat to low and keep broth at a simmer.

Melt 2 tablespoons butter in a large nonstick saucepan over medium heat. Add onions and garlic and sauté for 1½ minutes, stirring frequently, until onions are soft. Add rice and sauté, stirring constantly, for 1½ minutes, until edges of rice are transparent and centers are still white.

Add wine and stir until absorbed, about 1 minute. Add 1 cup warm broth and cook until liquid is absorbed but rice is not dry, stirring every 1–2 minutes. Repeat process, adding 3 more cups broth, 1 cup at a time, and stirring frequently until broth is absorbed. Then add remaining broth, ½ cup at a time, stirring frequently until liquid is absorbed. (Taste a kernel of rice between each addition of broth at this point to check consistency.)

When rice is tender on the outside but still al dente in the center, remove from heat. (Rice should be creamy, not soupy or dry, with a toothy center.) Cut remaining 2 tablespoons butter into small pieces. Stir butter and Parmesan cheese into risotto. Stir in ham, spinach, and tomatoes. Serve immediately. Sprinkle each serving with parsley.

 Prepare enhancements while broth is heating and risotto is cooking. Cut them into small, bite-size pieces. Some choices may need to be cooked or partially cooked before adding them to risotto (i.e. parboil vegetables such as asparagus until almost tender; sauté mushrooms until soft; sauté seafood, chicken, and meats until cooked through). For each 1 cup uncooked rice, you'll need approximately 3 cups liquid (plus ½ to 1 cup more for consistency adjustments).

Serves: 4–6 | 34 minutes

Southeast Asian Chicken Salad

Called nuoc mam *in Vietnam and* nam pla *in Thailand, fish sauce adds a special richness and saltiness to Asian recipes. Bottled in glass containers, the sauce will keep indefinitely if refrigerated.*

⅓ cup fish sauce

½ cup fresh lemon juice

¼ cup sugar

2 cloves garlic, minced

¼ teaspoon crushed red pepper flakes

5 cups coarsely chopped romaine lettuce hearts

1 delicatessen rotisserie chicken, meat removed from bones and chopped (about 4 cups)

1 heaping cup quartered grape tomatoes

1½ cups shredded carrots

1 cup chopped scallions

⅔ cup snipped fresh mint

Prepare the Asian dressing by placing fish sauce, lemon juice, sugar, garlic, and red pepper flakes in a small bowl. Stir until sugar is dissolved. Set aside.

Place lettuce, chicken, tomatoes, carrots, scallions, and mint in a large salad bowl. Toss gently with salad tongs to mix. Add half the Asian dressing and toss gently again. Add more dressing if desired so that ingredients are well coated.

 Using a rotisserie chicken guarantees easy preparation, but you can use any leftover chicken for this recipe. Shredded carrots are available in the produce section of most supermarkets if you do not want to prepare your own.

For a special presentation of this salad, buy small round bread loaves, cut off tops, and hollow out loaves (tearing bread as close to crust as possible). Brush inside of each loaf with 1 tablespoon sesame oil. Preheat oven to 425°F. Place loaves on oven rack and toast them for 10 minutes. Divide salad among bread bowls.

Serves: 6–8 | 20 minutes

Shrimp Waldorf Salad

Watch for sales of frozen shrimp at your supermarket or price club — often as low as $4 per pound — and stock up. You can buy precooked shrimp or cook your own. (To save time, look for shrimp already peeled and deveined.) Bring a pot of water to boil over high heat. Add 1 teaspoon seafood seasoning and shrimp and cook for 3 minutes, until shrimp just turn pink and start to curl up.

¾ cup mayonnaise
½ cup buttermilk
1½ tablespoons fresh lemon juice
1½ tablespoons snipped fresh tarragon
    or ½ teaspoon dried
1½ teaspoons Dijon mustard
Salt and freshly ground black pepper
1½ pounds cooked shrimp (51–60 count),
    peeled and deveined

3 cups chopped Fuji apples, cut into
    ¼-inch dice (about 2 apples)
3 cups halved red seedless grapes
2¼ cups chopped celery (cut into
    ¼-inch-dice)
½ cup slivered almonds, dry-toasted

Place mayonnaise, buttermilk, lemon juice, tarragon, and mustard in a medium bowl, and whisk to combine ingredients. Season dressing with salt and pepper to taste. Transfer to a covered container and refrigerate until needed.

Place shrimp in a large bowl. Add apples, grapes, celery, and almonds. Toss with just enough dressing to coat ingredients well. Season salad with salt and pepper to taste. Serve on a bed of lettuce leaves.

You can prepare most of the components of this salad up to 1 day ahead. Make dressing and refrigerate in a covered container until needed. Cook shrimp and refrigerate, covered with cooking liquid. Cut grapes and celery and toast the almonds. Place each ingredient in a small zipper bag and refrigerate until needed. Just before serving, cut up apples and combine them with the other ingredients in a large bowl. Toss with dressing and serve.

Fresh buttermilk has a short shelf life. Instead, purchase powdered buttermilk in the supermarket. You simply mix it with water. It is much more economical and you always will have it on hand.

Medium shrimp (51–60 count) cook up into bite-size pieces. If you use larger shrimp, cut them into ½-inch pieces after cooking.

Serves: 6 as a one-dish dinner (12 as part of a salad buffet) | 29 minutes

Baked Nachos

Sometimes a comforting meal is simply spelled n-a-c-h-o-s! And this recipe, loaded with protein and veggies, turns a guilty pleasure into a healthy choice.

1 cup refried beans
1 (10.75-ounce) can cheddar cheese soup
½ (13-ounce) bag restaurant-style white tortilla chips
1 (2.25-ounce) can sliced black olives, drained
1 cup chopped sweet onions, like Vidalia
1 cup diced tomatoes
¼ cup minced jalapeño peppers
1 (8-ounce) package shredded Colby and Monterey Jack cheese
Sour cream (optional)
Salsa (optional)
Guacamole (optional)

Preheat oven to 400°F. Place refried beans and cheese soup in a medium microwave-safe bowl and stir to combine. Microwave for 1½ minutes.

Meanwhile, place tortilla chips in a single, even layer on a large baking sheet. Place more chips strategically over any spaces between chips. Pour refried beans and cheese sauce over chips. Sprinkle olives, onions, tomatoes, and jalapeños atop cheese sauce layer. Top with shredded cheese.

Bake nachos for 5 minutes or until cheese has melted. Serve with sour cream, salsa, and guacamole, if desired.

 Use your imagination to change this recipe. Substitute diced cooked chicken for the refried beans. Use fresh salsa, drained of its liquid, instead of tomatoes. Or if you want to cool things down a bit, substitute a 4-ounce can chopped green chilies for the jalapeño peppers.

Serves: 4 for a meal; 8 for a snack | 22 minutes | 5 minutes

Farmers' Market

• Greens and Vegetables •

Salad Bowl

Caesar Salad

Crunchy Coleslaw

Spinach Salad with Warm Bacon Dressing

Corn and Black Bean Salad

Versatile Vegetables

Fried Green Tomatoes

Sautéed 'Shrooms

Caramelized Onions

Parmesan Spaghetti Squash

Salad Bowl

A wedge of iceberg lettuce topped with bottled blue cheese dressing may still be comfort food to many, but the twenty-first century salad bowl offers many more options. The wide availability of mixed baby greens and fresh herbs, specialty oils and vinegars, year-round veggies and fruits, and flavored cheeses, as well as a global array of seeds and nuts create a limitless palette from which to paint a salad masterpiece. You're the artist. Possibilities are endless. Combine your favorite blend of greens and chopped vegetables, add a little cheese, some toasted nuts or seeds, and maybe a sprinkling of fresh or dried fruits. Then toss it all together with a homemade salad dressing. Making your own fresh salad dressing is quick, easy, fun, and economical. The taste is superior to that of bottled dressings and more nutritious as well. Forget preservatives and chemical ingredients you can't identify. It will take you less than 10 minutes to mix up any one of the dressings offered here. Each makes enough to dress several large salads and will keep in the refrigerator for 1–2 weeks. And most cost less than $2 per batch.

BLUE CHEESE DRESSING

Okay, okay. It may be a bit pricier than the other salad dressings, but don't we all occasionally still yearn for a comforting wedge of iceberg lettuce topped with a thick glob of blue cheese dressing? Homemade is the best!

¼ cup mayonnaise

3 tablespoons sour cream

2 teaspoons milk

½ teaspoon Worcestershire sauce

1 tablespoon rice vinegar

1 teaspoon lemon juice

¼ teaspoon dry mustard

¼ teaspoon salt

¼ teaspoon black pepper

½ teaspoon sugar

½ cup crumbled blue cheese

Whisk mayonnaise, sour cream, and milk together in a medium bowl. Whisk in Worcestershire sauce, vinegar, lemon juice, dry mustard, salt, black pepper, and sugar. Add blue cheese and stir until creamy and well mixed. Transfer to a covered container and refrigerate until needed, up to 1 week. (If dressing gets too thick, thin by whisking in a little milk.) Makes about ¾ cup.

HONEY-MUSTARD VINAIGRETTE

You can substitute more exotic vinegars, such as chardonnay or champagne vinegar, in this recipe, if you have them on hand and your budget allows.

....

1 tablespoon Dijon mustard

2 tablespoons rice wine vinegar

2 tablespoons honey

¼ teaspoon salt

⅛ teaspoon ground white pepper

¼ cup extra-virgin olive oil

Place mustard, vinegar, honey, salt, and pepper in a small bowl. Beat with a wire whisk until well blended. Slowly add the olive oil, whisking constantly. Transfer to a covered container and refrigerate until needed. Makes about ½ cup.

RASPBERRY VINAIGRETTE

When raspberries are in season and reasonably priced, freeze them on parchment paper–lined baking sheets until solid, then pop them into labeled zipper bags and store them in the freezer until needed.

....

¼ cup fresh or frozen raspberries

2 tablespoons chopped onions

2 tablespoons rice wine vinegar

¼ teaspoon celery seed

1½ teaspoons dry mustard

¼ teaspoon salt

2 tablespoons plus 2 teaspoons honey

¼ cup extra-virgin olive oil

Place raspberries, onions, vinegar, celery seed, dry mustard, salt, and honey in a blender. Pulse until well mixed and raspberries are pureed. With blender on low, slowly add olive oil. Transfer dressing to a covered container and refrigerate until needed, up to 1 week. Makes about ¾ cup.

LEMON–POPPY SEED DRESSING

This light dressing is fantastic tossed with a salad of romaine lettuce, shredded Swiss cheese, cashews, dried cranberries, and diced apples and pears.

....

¼ cup sugar

¼ cup fresh lemon juice

1 teaspoon finely minced sweet onions, like Vidalia

½ teaspoon Dijon mustard

¼ teaspoon salt

⅓ cup olive oil

½ tablespoon poppy seeds

Place sugar, lemon juice, onions, mustard, and salt in a small mixing bowl. Whisk until sugar has dissolved. Slowly pour in olive oil, whisking constantly until mixture is smooth. Whisk in poppy seeds. Transfer to a covered container and refrigerate until needed, up to 1 week. Bring to room temperature before serving. Makes about ¾ cup.

Caesar Salad

Even people who don't like anchovies will enjoy this robust anchovy-infused Caesar dressing. The flavors are light, lemony, and well-balanced. For a dinner salad, top Caesar with sautéed shrimp, grilled boneless chicken breast strips, or stir-fried beef.

1 large egg
3½ tablespoons fresh lemon juice
1 tablespoon minced garlic
½ teaspoon Worcestershire sauce
1 tablespoon Dijon mustard
1 (2-ounce) can anchovies with oil
¾ cup olive oil

¼ cup plus 2 tablespoons grated
  Parmesan cheese
2 romaine lettuce hearts, washed, dried,
  and torn into bite-size pieces
Croutons
Freshly ground black pepper

Bring a small saucepan of water almost to a boil over high heat. Using a slotted spoon, lower egg into water for 45 seconds. Remove coddled egg and crack into a blender. Add lemon juice, garlic, Worcestershire sauce, mustard, and anchovies with their oil. Pulse mixture to blend well. With machine on low speed, slowly add olive oil. Add ¼ cup cheese and blend on slow speed until smooth. Transfer dressing to a covered container. (Makes about 1½ cups. The dressing will keep in the refrigerator for up to 2 weeks.)

Place lettuce in a large salad bowl. Drizzle with about ½ cup dressing and toss to coat. Add croutons and toss. Sprinkle salad with 2 tablespoons Parmesan cheese and season with freshly ground black pepper to taste.

 Recycle your stale bread into croutons. Preheat oven to 300°F. Coat both sides of bread slices with olive oil spray. Sprinkle with your favorite seasoning blend. Cut bread into cubes. Place a sheet of parchment paper on a baking sheet. Place bread cubes on paper. Bake for 8 minutes. Turn bread cubes and bake 8 minutes more, until cubes are dry and crispy. Cool and store in a covered container for up to a week or place in a zipper bag and freeze until needed. Prep time: 10 minutes. Bake time: 16 minutes.

Serves: 6 | 🍲 15 minutes

Crunchy Coleslaw

This recipe is equally tasty made with broccoli slaw and chopped broccoli florets instead of cabbage and red bell peppers. Or, try a mixture of all four ingredients — broccoli slaw, florets, cabbage slaw, and chopped red bell peppers — for a colorful, flavorful innovation.

1 package chicken-flavored ramen noodles
¼ cup slivered almonds
¼ cup sugar
¼ cup white vinegar
½ cup olive oil
1 (16-ounce) package 3-color cabbage slaw mixture
1 cup chopped red bell peppers
5 scallions, chopped
½ cup roasted sunflower seeds

Crush ramen noodles in package. Place almonds and ramen noodles (reserve seasoning packet) in 2 separate small skillets over medium-low heat. Toast nuts and noodles, stirring occasionally, until lightly browned, about 5 minutes. Set aside.

Meanwhile, place ramen noodle flavor packet, sugar, and vinegar in a small bowl. Whisk to combine. Slowly add olive oil, whisking constantly. Set aside until needed.

Place slaw, bell peppers, and scallions in a large bowl. Add toasted noodles, almonds, and sunflower seeds. Toss to combine. Pour dressing over salad to taste. Toss until mixture is well coated with dressing.

 To prepare in advance: Combine noodles, almonds, and sunflower seeds in a small zipper bag and set aside at room temperature. Combine slaw, bell peppers, and scallions in serving bowl; cover with plastic wrap; and refrigerate until needed. Prepare dressing and refrigerate in a covered container until needed. Just before serving, combine slaw mixture, noodle mixture, and dressing, and toss to combine. Double this recipe to feed a gang.

Serves: 6–8 | 🥘 15–18 minutes

Spinach Salad with Warm Bacon Dressing

A good source of iron and vitamins A and K, spinach became infamous as the canned vegetable Popeye loved and kids loved to hate. But both kids and the sailorman will love this fresh spinach salad, dressed with mushrooms and a warm, vinegary bacon dressing.

5 slices bacon

⅓ cup red wine vinegar

3 tablespoons orange juice

¼ cup honey

¼ teaspoon salt

⅛ teaspoon black pepper

1 (9-ounce) bag baby spinach, washed and spun dry

½ cup thinly sliced button mushrooms

¼ cup thinly sliced red onions

Cook bacon in a large nonstick skillet over medium heat until crispy. Remove bacon to drain on paper toweling. Reserve 1 tablespoon bacon grease in the skillet and discard the rest. Crumbled bacon and set aside.

Set the skillet over medium-low heat. Add vinegar, orange juice, honey, salt, and pepper. Cook until heated through, stirring occasionally, about 1 minute. Add crumbled bacon and cook 1 minute more.

Place spinach, mushrooms, and onions in a large salad bowl. Spoon dressing (to taste) over greens and toss to combine. Divide spinach among individual salad plates. Top with remaining crumbled bacon from dressing.

 This recipe makes ½ cup dressing. You won't need to use it all. You can prepare the dressing several hours ahead of time and refrigerate it in a covered container until needed. Microwave or reheat briefly on the stove until heated through before serving.

Serves: 4–6 | 🥣 20 minutes

Corn and Black Bean Salad

This multicolored salad tastes as bright and refreshing as it looks. It always adds pizzazz to an outdoor cookout. It is especially good when made with fresh sweet corn.

4 ears fresh sweet corn (shucked) or 2 cups frozen sweet corn

1 tablespoon sugar

1 (15-ounce) can black beans

4 scallions, chopped (about ½ cup)

½ cup chopped orange bell pepper

½ cup chopped seeded tomato

2 tablespoons fresh dill weed or 2 teaspoons dried

1 teaspoon garlic paste or finely minced garlic

3 tablespoons apple cider vinegar

¼ cup olive oil

Salt and freshly ground black pepper

Bring a large pot of water to boil over medium heat. Add fresh sweet corn and sugar. Reduce heat to medium and cook for 5 minutes. Drain corn, rinse, and drain again. If you are using frozen corn, cook according to package instructions.

While water is coming to boil and corn is cooking, rinse and drain black beans and chop vegetables. Place beans and chopped vegetables in a large bowl.

In a small bowl, whisk together dill, garlic, and vinegar. Slowly add olive oil, whisking constantly.

Cut sweet corn from cob. Add to beans and vegetables in bowl. Drizzle dressing over vegetables and toss to combine. Serve immediately or transfer to a covered container and refrigerate until needed (up to 2 days).

 This salad actually gets better the longer it sits, so it is a great recipe to make ahead.

Serves: 6–8 | 🥘 25 minutes

Versatile Vegetables

A perfectly steamed vegetable, tossed or drizzled with a tasty sauce, adds a flavorful, healthful boost to any meal. Below you'll find four versatile vegetables and four yummy topper sauces. Mix and match any way you choose. All combos are much less than $2 per serving and can be prepared in 15 minutes or fewer. All sauces can be made ahead and refrigerated until needed. Reheat on low heat or microwave for 30 seconds to 1 minute before serving.

ASPARAGUS

Asparagus deteriorates fairly quickly. Wrap damp paper toweling around its stems and store in a plastic zipper bag in the refrigerator. It will last several days. Clean asparagus under running water, bending the stalks until each naturally snaps. Discard the woody ends. Large asparagus, which is more mature and less tender, may need to be peeled with a vegetable peeler.

To steam: Place asparagus in a medium skillet. Cover with water. Place skillet over medium-high heat and cook about 3 minutes (thin asparagus), or until crisp-tender when tested with a fork. Remove from heat. Drain, rinse with cold water, and drain again.

Place asparagus on a serving platter. Drizzle with choice of sauces (opposite). Serve asparagus hot or at room temperature.

GREEN BEANS

Place cleaned beans in a vegetable steamer over 2 inches of water in a large saucepan. Steam beans over medium-high heat for 5 minutes, or until beans are crisp-tender when tested with a fork. Drain, rinse with cold water, and drain again.

Place green beans on a serving platter. Drizzle with choice of sauces (opposite).

BABY CARROTS

Cut baby carrots in quarters, lengthwise. Place carrots with water to cover in a medium saucepan over high heat. When water comes to a boil, reduce heat to medium. Cook for 8–10 minutes, until carrots are cooked through but still slightly crunchy. Drain, rinse with cold water, and drain again. Return carrots to saucepan and toss with choice of sauces (opposite).

Place dressed carrots on a serving platter.

SUGAR SNAP PEAS

Cut stem ends from sugar snap peas. Place a large saucepan of water over high heat. When water comes to a boil, add peas. Cook for 30 seconds only. Drain, rinse with cold water, and drain again. Place peas in a serving bowl and toss with choice of sauces (opposite).

Sauces

GINGER-HOISIN SAUCE

2 tablespoons rice wine vinegar

1 tablespoon gingerroot paste or finely grated fresh gingerroot

2 tablespoons hoisin sauce

¼ cup chopped scallions

Place vinegar, gingerroot, hoisin sauce, and scallions in a small bowl. Whisk to mix. You can prepare the ginger-hoisin sauce up to 3 days ahead. Place in a covered container and refrigerate until needed. Bring sauce to room temperature before drizzling on hot veggies. Makes ⅓ cup | 🍲 3½ minutes

SESAME-ORANGE SAUCE

1½ tablespoons sesame seeds

¼ cup frozen orange juice concentrate, thawed

2 tablespoons Dijon mustard

⅓ cup red currant jelly

1½ tablespoons red wine vinegar

Dash cayenne pepper

1½ tablespoons olive oil

Place sesame seeds in a small skillet over medium-low heat until lightly toasted, about 2 minutes. Shake pan occasionally.

Meanwhile, place orange juice concentrate, mustard, jelly, vinegar, and pepper in a small saucepan over medium-low heat. Whisk until jelly has melted and mixture is bubbly. Remove from heat and whisk in oil and sesame seeds. Drizzle over steamed vegetables. Makes ¾ cup | 🍲 5 minutes

LEMON-MUSTARD SAUCE

3 tablespoons butter

1½ teaspoons fresh lemon juice

1½ teaspoons Dijon mustard

Melt butter in microwave for 1 minute. Whisk in lemon juice and mustard. Drizzle over steamed vegetables. Makes ¼ cup | 🍲 4 minutes

FRESH HERB AND BUTTER SAUCE

4 tablespoons (½ stick) butter

½ cup minced sweet onions, like Vidalia

½ teaspoon garlic paste or finely minced garlic

¼ cup finely minced celery

½ cup snipped fresh parsley

1 teaspoon snipped fresh rosemary

1 teaspoon snipped fresh basil

¼ teaspoon kosher salt

Melt butter in a medium nonstick skillet over medium heat. Add onions, garlic, and celery. Sauté until onions are soft but celery is still slightly crunchy, about 3 minutes. Stir in parsley, rosemary, basil, and salt, and cook for 1 minute more. Drizzle over steamed vegetables. Makes ½ cup | 🍲 10 minutes

Fried Green Tomatoes

A Southern summertime favorite, fried green tomatoes stormed the national stage with the release of the 1991 movie of the same name. This is a great way to showcase the end-of-the-season tomato harvest.

3 tablespoons flour
¼ cup Italian seasoned dry bread crumbs
3 tablespoons shredded Parmesan cheese
⅛ teaspoon cayenne pepper
1 egg
¼ cup milk
3 tablespoons canola oil
2 large green tomatoes, cut into ⅜-inch slices (8 slices)
Salt and freshly ground black pepper

Mix flour, bread crumbs, Parmesan cheese, and cayenne pepper together in a shallow bowl. In a separate shallow bowl, whisk egg and milk together to form an egg wash.

Heat oil in a large nonstick skillet over medium heat. Dip each tomato slice in egg wash, coating both sides. Press each egg-wash-coated tomato slice into bread crumb mixture, coating both sides evenly. Place breaded tomato slices in hot oil in skillet. Reduce heat to medium-low. Cook tomatoes for 3 minutes or until undersides are golden brown. Turn tomato slices with a firm spatula. Cook for 2–3 more minutes or until undersides are golden brown. Season with salt and pepper to taste. Serve immediately.

For a great vegetarian sandwich to accompany a bowl of soup, place a fried green tomato slice and a crisp lettuce leaf in a toasted hamburger bun spread with wasabi mayonnaise or aïoli (garlic mayonnaise).

Serves: 4 | 11 minutes | 6 minutes

Sautéed 'Shrooms

These sautéed mushrooms will forever evoke memories of the two years I lived in Boston's North End, where our local salumeria (Italian deli) prepared them expertly. Serve this pure Italian comfort food on a crusty roll for a vegetarian sandwich or with Steak on the Grill (page 69).

½ pound white button mushroom caps

½ pound brown button mushroom caps

¼ pound fresh shiitake mushrooms (optional)

6 ounces portobello mushroom caps

5 tablespoons olive oil, divided

3 cloves garlic, minced

½ teaspoon salt

½ teaspoon black pepper

3 tablespoons balsamic vinegar

Remove stems from all mushrooms and scrape gills from portobellos with a kitchen spoon. Using a wet paper towel, wipe clean all mushroom caps. Cut button mushroom caps in half (cut large mushrooms into quarters). Leave small shiitake caps whole, but cut large caps in half. Cut portobello caps in half and then slice into 1-inch-wide pieces.

Heat 2 tablespoons olive oil in a large nonstick skillet over medium-high heat. Add garlic and sauté for about 30 seconds. Add mushrooms and sauté, stirring frequently, for 2 minutes. Add 2 tablespoons olive oil and continue cooking and stirring for 3 minutes more. Add final tablespoon oil and cook 1 minute longer.

Sprinkle mushrooms with salt and pepper and add balsamic vinegar. Sauté, stirring constantly, for 1 minute.

 Shiitake mushrooms, which have a rich, steaklike flavor, are pricey (about $8.00 for ¼ pound). Use them in this recipe for a special occasion if your budget allows. Otherwise use another quarter pound of button mushrooms.

Serves: 6–8 | 17 minutes | 🕐 7 minutes

93

Caramelized Onions

The few extra minutes it takes to make caramelized onions are worth the effort (and you can refrigerate them in a covered container for up to 3 days). The relatively slow cooking and sprinkling of sugar make the onions sweet and satisfying.

2 large sweet onions, like Vidalia

1 tablespoon olive oil

2 teaspoons sugar

Peel onions and cut into ¼-inch-thick slices. Heat oil in a large nonstick skillet over medium-low heat. Add onions and sauté, stirring occasionally, for 18 minutes, or until onions are lightly browned. Sprinkle sugar over onions and sauté for 5 minutes more, stirring frequently.

 Serve these onions with Steak on the Grill (page 69), pile them on a grilled burger (page 27), or add them to a homemade pizza (page 32).

Serves: 4–6 | 5 minutes | 🕐 23 minutes

Parmesan Spaghetti Squash

When the leaves start turning and the air turns brisk, this warm, buttery spaghetti squash is at the forefront of my comfort food repertoire. The flavors transcend the ingredients in this recipe.

1 (1½-pound) spaghetti squash
4 tablespoons (½ stick) butter
½ cup chopped sweet onions, like Vidalia
¼ teaspoon kosher salt
¼ teaspoon cracked black pepper
¼ cup grated Parmesan cheese

Cut squash in half and scoop out seeds and membranes. Place each half, cut side down, in a microwave dish large enough to accommodate squash and still turn easily on microwave turntable. Microwave squash for 13 minutes, or until skin has softened to the touch.

While squash is cooking, melt butter in a small skillet over medium heat. Add onions and sauté, stirring frequently for 1 minute, until onions have softened. Remove from heat.

Using a fork, scrape strands of spaghetti squash into a serving dish. Add butter and onions and toss to combine. Sprinkle with salt, pepper, and cheese, and toss again.

 The oval-shaped spaghetti squash comes in many sizes. This is probably as small as you'll find; some grow to 3 pounds or more. For larger squash, follow directions above, but microwave only a half at a time. Increase amounts of butter, onions, and seasonings based on the size of the squash.

You can use spaghetti squash as a low-carb, low-cal substitute for regular spaghetti. Spaghetti squash has 10g carbs per cup compared with 40g per cup for spaghetti. Top squash with marinara sauce and serve with Neapolitan-style Meatballs (page 50).

Serves: 4 | 10 minutes | 13 minutes

Side Shows

• Potatoes, Rice, Beans, and Breads •

Mashed Menagerie

Slow Cooker Baked Potatoes

Cheesy Baked Hash Browns

German Potato Salad

Maple-Glazed Sweet Potatoes

Herbed Tomato Orzo

Slow Cooker Baked Beans

Rice, Rice, and More Rice

Cheese Bread

Cheddar Bay Biscuits

Orange Monkey Bread

Mashed Menagerie

Mashed potatoes hit the big time when they began starring on trendy restaurant menus. These quick and easy recipes bring the spuds back to their roots — the home kitchen — where mashed potatoes have always reigned as supreme comfort food.

REAL DEAL GARLIC MASHED POTATOES

The secret to fluffy, lump-free mashed potatoes is a potato ricer. It is easy to use and inexpensive to purchase. The ricer paddle forces the potato pieces through a mesh of little holes. Unlike mashing with a hand-masher or electric mixer beaters, the ricer barely damages the potato's starch cells, which results in a lighter, fluffier texture.

4 cups Yukon Gold potatoes cut into 2-inch cubes

4 whole peeled garlic cloves

2 teaspoons salt, divided

3 tablespoons butter, cut into ½-inch cubes

3 tablespoons half-and-half, warmed in microwave for 30 seconds

½ teaspoon freshly ground black pepper

Place potatoes and garlic cloves in a large saucepan with water to cover. Add 1 teaspoon salt, cover pan, and bring to a boil over high heat. Reduce heat to medium-high and cook, uncovered, until tender, about 10 minutes. Drain potatoes and return to the pan for 30 seconds.

Squeeze potatoes and garlic through a potato ricer. Add butter, half-and-half, 1 teaspoon salt, and black pepper. Stir gently to combine ingredients. Serve immediately.

 You can refrigerate potatoes in a covered container until needed and make baked mashed potatoes by following the recipe on the opposite page. Bring potatoes to room temperature before baking. Increase baking time to 20 minutes.

Serves: 4 (¾ cup per serving) | 15 minutes | 15 minutes

SUPER SPEEDY MASHED POTATOES

Potato purists will gasp at this recipe, but these mashed potatoes — commercially flavored with butter, sour cream, cheese, bacon, onion, and chives, and enhanced with a creamy jolt of sour cream — are speedy, cheap, and very, very, tasty.

1 (4-ounce) package Idahoan Loaded Baked Mashed Potatoes mix
½ cup sour cream

Just before serving, place 2 cups boiling water in serving bowl. Add mashed potato mix all at once and stir with a fork to moisten. Allow potatoes to rest for I minute. Add sour cream and stir to combine well. Serve immediately with butter or gravy.

 Instant potatoes have come a long, long way in the past 40 years. This brand includes a number of different mashed potato mixes that you can jazz up with your own additions of herbs, cheeses, and flavorings such as minced ham or bacon.

Serves: 4 | 5 minutes

ALMOST TWICE-BAKED POTATOES

This knockoff of traditional twice-baked potatoes eliminates all the muss and fuss without sacrificing any of the creamy, cheesy comfort.

1 (4-ounce) package Idahoan Four Cheese Mashed Potatoes mix
½ cup sour cream ranch dip, like T. Marzetti
1 cup shredded sharp cheddar, Swiss, or mozzarella cheese

Preheat oven to 350°F. Place 2 cups boiling water in a medium mixing bowl. Add mashed potato mix all at once and stir with a fork to moisten. Allow potatoes to rest for I minute. Add ranch dip and stir to combine well.

Coat the insides of 4 (3-inch) ramekins with vegetable cooking spray. Spoon mashed potatoes equally into the 4 dishes. Top each with ¼ cup shredded cheese. Bake for 10 minutes, until potatoes are heated through and cheese has melted.

 Sprinkle potatoes with bacon or chives, or change the flavor of these faux twice-baked potatoes by substituting another flavor dip, such as onion or Southwestern-style.

Serves: 4 | 7 minutes | 🕐 10 minutes

Slow Cooker Baked Potatoes

Baked potatoes are one of the easiest things to prepare in any cook's arsenal of comfort food, but they take at least an hour in a hot oven to be great. Microwaving a potato cuts time, but it also cuts flavor. This recipe for baked potatoes — cooked in the slow cooker — bridges the gap. So when you don't have an extra hour at mealtime, load up your slow cooker in the morning and go about your life. The resulting taste and texture of the potatoes rivals that of oven-baked.

4 extra-large (1-pound) russet baking potatoes, washed and dried

Olive oil spray

McCormick Garlic Herb Seasoning Blend or seasoning of choice

Coat potatoes with olive oil spray. Sprinkle seasoning over all sides of potatoes. Prick potatoes in about 6 places with a fork. Place in slow cooker and cook on low for 8–10 hours. (Potatoes will be done in 8 hours, but will hold for 2 hours more.)

Serve with butter, sour cream, bacon bits, and/or chives. Or make an easy whole meal out of the potatoes by loading them with leftovers from one of this book's saucy recipes: Sloppy Joes, Beef and Bean Chili, Chicken Puttanesca, Hamburger Stroganoff, Turkey Taco Melts, or Pasta Bolognese.

 To bake potatoes in a 375°F oven, pierce them in several places with a fork so that the steam escapes. Bake for 1½ hours.

Serves: 4 | 8 minutes | 🕐 7–8 hours

Cheesy Baked Hash Browns

These are great potatoes to serve a large group. The recipe will serve 12 when prepared in a 9x13-inch baking dish. I've offered the option to divide the recipe into 2 portions and freeze half for use at another meal.

1 (30-ounce) package Country-Style Hash Brown shredded potatoes, thawed

2 cups (1 pint) sour cream

1 (8-ounce) package Sargento Authentic Mexican Artisan Blend shredded cheese

1 cup chopped sweet onions, like Vidalia

3 tablespoons milk

1 teaspoon kosher salt

1 teaspoon cracked black pepper

⅔ cup fresh bread crumbs

4 tablespoons (½ stick) butter, melted

Preheat oven to 375°F. Mix potatoes, sour cream, shredded cheese, onions, milk, salt, and pepper together in a large bowl. Coat 2 (8x8-inch) baking dishes with vegetable cooking spray. Divide potato mixture evenly between the 2 dishes.

Place bread crumbs in a medium bowl. Pour melted butter over crumbs and stir with a fork to coat crumbs evenly. Sprinkle the buttered crumbs evenly over the potato mixture in each dish. Place one dish in the oven and bake, uncovered, for 45 minutes. Cover other dish with plastic wrap, then aluminum foil, and freeze until needed. Thaw before baking.

Sargento-brand Authentic Mexican Blend shredded cheese is a combination of queso quesadilla, asadero, queso gallego, manchego, and anejo enchilada cheeses. You'll find it comparably priced to cheddar or mozzarella in the shredded cheese section of your supermarket. You can substitute your favorite shredded cheese if you like.

Serves: 12 (6 servings per dish) | 12 minutes | 35–40 minutes

German Potato Salad

My favorite aunt, Fern, learned this heirloom recipe from my German grandmother and has preserved it for the ages. The warm bacon dressing with vinegar sets it apart from other versions of potato salad. The flavors get better when they marry for a few days, so this is a great salad to make ahead and reheat.

8 medium (2½-inch diameter) Yukon Gold potatoes, cut in quarters
8 slices bacon, cut into ½-inch pieces
¼ cup flour
5 tablespoons white vinegar
¾ cup sugar
1 cup chopped celery
¾ cup chopped sweet onions, like Vidalia
Salt and freshly ground black pepper

Place potatoes in a large pot with water to cover. Boil potatoes until cooked through but still firm, about 15 minutes. Drain potatoes; peel and cut them into ¼-inch-thick slices.

While potatoes are boiling, place bacon in a large frying pan over medium heat and fry until crispy. Remove bacon with a slotted spoon and place it on paper toweling to drain. Reserve ¼ cup bacon grease in pan; discard the rest. Stir flour into bacon grease. Add 1½ cups water, vinegar, and sugar. Stir over medium heat until mixture is smooth and sugar is dissolved.

Add celery, onions, potatoes, and cooked bacon pieces. Stir to mix well. Season with salt and pepper to taste. Reduce heat to medium-low and simmer, stirring frequently, for 15 minutes.

 You can prepare potato salad up to 2 days ahead. Cook for only 5 minutes. Transfer potato salad to a covered container and refrigerate until needed. Reheat potato salad in a large skillet over medium-low heat for 15 minutes or until heated through.

Serves: 6 | 20 minutes | 15 minutes

Maple-Glazed Sweet Potatoes

These rich, sweet, crunchy sweet potato chunks are not your mama's marshmallow-topped, brown-sugared sweet potato casserole — they are better! Don't wait for Thanksgiving to serve them.

2 pounds sweet potatoes
4 tablespoons (½ stick) butter
½ cup maple syrup
¼ cup glazed pecans

Peel sweet potatoes. Cut each potato in quarters lengthwise, then slice them crosswise into ½-inch slices.

Melt butter in a large skillet over medium heat. Add sweet potatoes and toss to coat evenly with butter. Add maple syrup and bring to a boil, stirring frequently, for 10 minutes. Reduce heat to medium low and continue cooking, stirring frequently, for 5 minutes. Reduce heat to low, add pecans, and cook, stirring frequently, until potatoes are glazed and cooked through, but still firm, about 3 minutes.

Glazed pecans are commonly marketed by Emerald brand, found in the peanut/cashew section of the supermarket. If you can't find glazed pecans, you can use regular pecans. Toast them first in a dry skillet over medium-low heat. They won't be as sweet, but they make an adequate substitute.

Serves: 4–6 | 10 minutes | 20 minutes

Herbed Tomato Orzo

Orzo is actually tiny pasta shaped like grains of rice. It cooks quickly like pasta, but has the texture of Arborio or risotto rice. This dish is equally good warm or at room temperature. It will keep in the refrigerator for days — the flavors just keep getting better and better.

1 cup uncooked orzo

2 medium tomatoes

2 tablespoons olive oil

½ teaspoon cracked pepper

¼ teaspoon salt

⅓ cup snipped fresh basil

1½ tablespoons snipped fresh dill

½ cup (4-ounces) crumbled tomato-basil feta cheese

Bring a large pot of water to boil over high heat. Add orzo and cook to al dente, about 8 minutes. Drain orzo.

While orzo is cooking, seed and dice tomatoes. Place tomatoes, olive oil, pepper, salt, basil, dill, and feta cheese in a large bowl. Add drained orzo. Toss to mix well. Serve warm or refrigerate until needed. Serve at room temperature.

 To seed tomatoes, cut them in half horizontally. Holding each tomato half over sink, scoop out seeds with your fingers. Drain tomatoes on paper toweling.

For a dinner party presentation: Up to 3 hours ahead, cut the tops off 6 medium tomatoes and scoop out the pulp. Chop the tomato pulp, tops, and another portion of tomato to make 1 cup. Proceed with recipe, then stuff each tomato with the orzo mixture. Bake tomatoes for 15 minutes at 325°F.

Serves: 8 | 20 minutes

Slow Cooker Baked Beans

Campbell's beware. This potpourri of full-flavored, slow-cooked legumes redefines baked beans. Serve these baked beans as a hearty side dish, or pair them with steamed or recycled rice for a protein-rich meal (see Steamed Rice recipe, page 106).

6 slices bacon, cut in ½-inch dice

5 cloves garlic, minced

¾ cup chopped sweet onions, like Vidalia

1 tablespoon Worcestershire sauce

2 tablespoons cider vinegar

¾ cup ketchup

3 heaping tablespoons dark brown sugar

1 teaspoon dry mustard

2 (14-ounce) cans pork and beans

1 (16-ounce) can chick peas or red kidney beans, rinsed and drained

1 (15.5-ounce) can butter beans, rinsed and drained

1 (15.25-ounce) can baby lima beans, rinsed and drained

Fry bacon in a large nonstick skillet over medium heat until cooked through but not crispy. Remove with a slotted spoon and drain bacon on paper toweling. Reserve 1 tablespoon bacon grease in skillet; discard the rest.

Place garlic and onions in skillet and sauté over medium heat, stirring frequently, for about 1½ minutes, until onions are soft but not brown. Reduce heat to medium-low. Add Worcestershire sauce, vinegar, ketchup, brown sugar, and dry mustard. Stir to mix well. Cook mixture, stirring constantly, for 1½ minutes. Remove from heat.

Place pork and beans, chick peas, butter beans, and lima beans in a slow cooker. Add bacon and onion sauce mixture. Stir to mix until beans are well coated with sauce. Cover slow cooker and cook for 6 hours on low or 3 hours on high.

 To freeze individual slices of uncooked bacon, lay them out on a piece of waxed paper, then roll them up. There will be a piece of waxed paper between each piece and you can simply peel off individual slices as you need them.

Serves: 8–10 | 21 minutes | 3–6 hours

Rice, Rice, and More Rice

Rice is best prepared in large quantities, which is great because it freezes very well. I always make a big pot of steamed rice and then freeze the leftovers in 2- to 3-cup plastic containers for later use, such as recycled rice pilafs and cold rice salads (see following recipes).

STEAMED RICE

Turmeric replaces saffron in this recipe. Saffron is the world's most expensive spice. Each strand is the stigma of a saffron crocus flower, which must be harvested by hand. It takes 80,000 stigmas to make a pound of saffron, but only a few strands to flavor and color a dish. Turmeric, the cheaper alternative, adds the distinctive golden tint to the rice, but it will not impart any flavor.

2 cups basmati or other long-grain rice

2 tablespoons butter

¼ teaspoon ground turmeric (optional)

4 cups water or chicken broth

¼ teaspoon salt

¼ teaspoon black pepper

Place rice in a medium bowl. Cover rice with water and, with clean hands, agitate the rice, releasing the starch. Pour off the cloudy water and repeat this process until the water is clear. Drain rice in a colander.

Melt butter in a large saucepan over medium heat. Add rinsed rice and turmeric and sauté, stirring frequently, for 3 minutes. Add water or broth, salt, and pepper. Stir to combine.

Bring to a boil, stirring frequently. Reduce heat to low, cover, and simmer, undisturbed, for 20 minutes, until liquid is absorbed. Remove from heat and fluff rice with a fork. Place 3 pieces of paper toweling over saucepan and replace lid. Allow rice to rest for 5 minutes or until needed. (The paper toweling will absorb the steam, ensuring that the rice is light and the kernels separate.) Recipe makes 6 cups steamed rice.

  For coconut-flavored rice, use jasmine rice instead of basmati, eliminate the turmeric, and substitute 2 cups coconut milk and 2 cups water for the liquid in this recipe.

Serves: 8 | 10 minutes | 20 minutes | Rest time: 5 minutes

PEANUT-RAISIN RECYCLED RICE PILAF

Add bite-size pieces of leftover meat or poultry to turn this recipe into a one-dish dinner.

4 tablespoons (½ stick) butter

1 cup chopped sweet onions, like Vidalia

½ cup chopped peanuts

½ cup raisins

3 cups cooked rice

¼ teaspoon kosher salt

½ teaspoon cracked black pepper

Melt butter in a large nonstick skillet over medium heat. Add onions and sauté 2 minutes, stirring occasionally. Reduce heat to medium-low and add peanuts and raisins. Sauté for 2 minutes. Add rice and toss well with other ingredients. Add salt and pepper. Reduce heat to low and cook, stirring frequently, for 5–6 minutes, until rice is heated through and flavors have married.

 Substitute dried cranberries, cherries, or currants for the raisins. Or try cashews, almonds, or pine nuts instead of the peanuts. You can further jazz up recycled rice with fresh herbs, like snipped dill, parsley, or basil, or you can add veggies such as chopped bell peppers, tomatoes, green chilies, black beans, or corn.

Serves: 6 | 10 minutes | 10 minutes

SPINACH RICE SALAD

You can toss leftover steamed rice with the dressing up to 2 hours ahead if you like. Prepare the spinach, celery, bacon, and scallions ahead also. Then toss these ingredients with the dressed rice just before serving.

5 slices smoked bacon

½ cup Marie's Creamy Italian Garlic Dressing

1 tablespoon soy sauce

½ teaspoon sugar

3 cups cold cooked rice

2 cups fresh spinach cut into thin strips

½ cup sliced celery

½ cup sliced scallions, including tops

Cook bacon in a large nonstick skillet over medium heat until crispy. Drain on paper toweling and crumble. Mix dressing, soy sauce, and sugar together in a small bowl. Place rice in a large bowl. Add dressing and toss to combine. Add spinach, celery, crumbled bacon, and scallions. Toss to combine. Serve immediately.

 If you can't find Marie's Creamy Italian Garlic Dressing, substitute Marie's Ranch Dressing.

Serves: 6-8 | 21 minutes

Cheese Bread

Rich and gooey with cheese, this bread is a wonderful accompaniment for a dinner salad meal or a plate of pasta (see recipes in One Dish Dinners and Oodles of Noodles chapters).

8 tablespoons (1 stick) butter, softened
2 tablespoons mayonnaise
1 tablespoon Dijon mustard
1 tablespoon lemon juice
2 teaspoons dried onion flakes
1 loaf Italian bread
1¼ cups shredded Swiss cheese

Preheat oven to 375°F. Place butter, mayonnaise, mustard, lemon juice, and onion flakes in a small bowl. Stir to mix well.

Slice bread into 1-inch-thick pieces. Spread butter mixture on one side of each bread slice, then sprinkle with cheese and press it into the butter. Reassemble the slices into a loaf, buttered side against unbuttered side. Place loaf on a double piece of aluminum foil on a baking sheet. Bend foil around lower loaf to hold slices in place but don't completely encase the bread in foil.

Place bread in preheated oven and bake, uncovered, for 10–15 minutes, until the cheese is melted and the bread crust is crisp.

 You can prepare the butter mixture up to 3 days ahead. Cover and refrigerate until needed. Allow butter to stand at room temperature until softened, about 30 minutes. You can also assemble the bread loaf up to 1 hour ahead. Cover it loosely with a piece of aluminum foil until ready to bake.

Serves: 8 | 15 minutes | 🕐 10–15 minutes

Cheddar Bay Biscuits

Red Lobster restaurant chain bakes more than 395 million Cheddar Bay Biscuits a year. You can bake these tasty knockoffs in only 10 minutes. They are great with soup, salad, seafood, or pasta.

1 (8-ounce) package Jiffy Buttermilk Biscuit Mix
⅓ cup whole milk
1 cup shredded sharp cheddar cheese
1 tablespoon butter, melted
⅛ teaspoon garlic powder
Dried parsley

Preheat oven to 450°F. Place biscuit mix, milk, and cheese in a medium bowl. Stir to combine. Coat a baking sheet with vegetable cooking spray. Drop batter by kitchen tablespoonfuls onto baking sheet, 2 inches apart. Bake for 8–10 minutes, or until golden.

Meanwhile, mix melted butter and garlic powder together in a small bowl. Brush on tops of baked biscuits. Sprinkle with dried parsley.

 Substitute mild cheddar cheese if you don't like the stronger taste of the sharp. Create your own Bay Biscuits by substituting pepper jack or another flavored cheese.

Serves: 6 (2 biscuits per serving) | 10 minutes | 🕐 10 minutes

Orange Monkey Bread

This is a lighter, citrus version of the ever-popular caramel monkey bread. Easily assembled the night before and baked in minutes in the morning, the pull-apart orange-glazed rolls make a great breakfast or brunch accompaniment.

5 tablespoons butter, melted, plus 1 tablespoon hard butter

1 cup sugar

Grated rind from 1 orange

3 tablespoons fresh-squeezed orange juice

1 (15-count) package Rhodes or other frozen dough rolls

The night before: Generously butter a 9x13-inch baking dish with 1 tablespoon hard butter. Mix melted butter, sugar, orange rind, and orange juice together in a small bowl. Pour into buttered pan. Place dough rolls atop orange mixture.

Coat a sheet of waxed paper with vegetable cooking spray. Place paper over rolls in baking dish. Leave dish on kitchen counter overnight.

In the morning: Preheat oven to 350°F. Discard waxed paper. Bake monkey bread for 20–25 minutes. With a firm spatula, remove monkey bread from oven and flip over onto serving platter. Drizzle any remaining orange mixture over monkey bread. Serve immediately.

 One of a cook's best investments is a microplane grater, available at most stores that sell kitchenware. You can grate orange or lemon peel in mere seconds. Buy a bag of fresh citrus. Grate the peel from the citrus and then freeze this zest, wrapped in plastic wrap. Juice the fruit and freeze in ½-cup containers for future use. You'll have grated citrus peel and fresh citrus juice on hand for months.

Serves: 10 | 10 minutes | 20–25 minutes

Sweet Eats

• Sundaes, Cookies, and Desserts •

Over the Top Ice Cream Sauces

The Ultimate Comfort Cookies

Fudge Nutty Brownies

Grand Marnier Strawberry-Almond Shortcake

Death by Chocolate Mousse Trifle

Peach Cobbler

Apple Tart

Pumpkin Satin Pie

Key Lime Pie

Southern Banana Pudding

Blackberry Cheesecake Bites

Cherry-Fudge Babycakes

Orange Rum Cake

Butter-Pecan Bundt Cake

Over the Top Ice Cream Sauces

When your sweet tooth calls for ice cream, here is the answer. Whether you prefer a banana split or an ice cream sundae, you are sure to love these homemade sauces. Choose hot fudge, butterscotch, or mixed berry sauce — or all three — and create your own masterpiece.

HOT FUDGE SAUCE

8 tablespoons butter (in 8 pieces)
6 (1-ounce) squares unsweetened chocolate
1 cup evaporated milk
2½ cups confectioners' sugar
1 teaspoon vanilla

Place about 3 inches water in the bottom of a double boiler. Place butter and chocolate in top of double boiler. Place double boiler over high heat, covered, and melt butter and chocolate, stirring frequently, about 10 minutes. When both are melted, reduce heat to medium-low and add evaporated milk and sugar. Stir to combine and cook for 5 minutes, stirring constantly, until sugar is melted and sauce is smooth. Remove pan from heat and stir in vanilla. Transfer to a covered container and refrigerate until needed. Warm sauce in microwave for 30–45 seconds before serving or serve sauce at room temperature.

 Hot fudge sauce will keep for months in the refrigerator.

Makes: 3 cups (12 ¼-cup servings) | 2 minutes | 15 minutes

BUTTERSCOTCH SAUCE

3 tablespoons butter

¼ cup light corn syrup

⅔ cup firmly packed light brown sugar

Pinch of salt

⅓ cup evaporated milk

Pinch of baking soda

1 teaspoon vanilla

Place butter, corn syrup, brown sugar, and salt in a medium saucepan over medium heat. Cook, stirring frequently, until butter is melted, about 2½ minutes. When mixture comes to a boil, reduce heat to low, and simmer for 2 minutes, stirring occasionally, until sugar is dissolved. Meanwhile, mix evaporated milk, baking soda, and vanilla together in a small bowl. Add milk mixture and cook for 1½ minutes more, stirring constantly, until sauce is smooth and well mixed. Remove pan from heat and cool for 5 minutes. Transfer to a covered container and refrigerate until needed. Warm sauce in microwave for 30–45 seconds before serving.

You can use dark brown sugar in a pinch. Sauce will keep for months in the refrigerator.

Makes: 1 cup (4 ¼-cup servings) | 4 minutes | 6 minutes (+ 5 minutes to cool)

ALL BERRY SAUCE

1 (16-ounce) package frozen mixed berries

⅓ cup firmly packed dark brown sugar

2 tablespoons fresh lemon juice

2 tablespoons crème de cassis (black currant liqueur) or blackberry syrup (optional)

Dash of ground cinnamon

Place frozen berries, brown sugar, lemon juice, and liqueur or syrup in a medium saucepan over medium heat. Stir to combine and cook mixture for 4 minutes, stirring frequently, until sugar dissolves and berries soften. Reduce heat to medium-low and simmer for 6 minutes, stirring occasionally. Remove from heat and cool for 5 minutes. Transfer to a covered container and refrigerate until needed. Warm sauce in microwave for 30–45 seconds before serving or serve sauce cold or at room temperature.

Frozen mixed berries include strawberries, blueberries, blackberries, and raspberries. You can substitute 4 cups of seasonal fresh berries if you like.

Makes: 2 cups (8 ¼-cup servings) | 5 minutes | 10 minutes (+ 5 minutes to cool)

The Ultimate Comfort Cookies

Nothing is more comforting than warm homemade cookies, right from the oven, and these giant cookies showcase all the comfort cookie food groups — peanut butter, oatmeal, raisins, and chocolate chips — in one yummy recipe. Bake a dozen and freeze the rest of the dough to bake up fresh in 18 minutes when the spirit moves you.

2 cups sifted flour	2 large eggs
1 teaspoon salt	1 teaspoon vanilla
1 teaspoon ground cinnamon	¼ cup milk
1 teaspoon baking soda	1 cup raisins
12 tablespoons (1½ sticks) butter	1½ cups quick-cooking oats
½ cup chunky peanut butter	1 cup semisweet chocolate chips
1 cup brown sugar	1 tablespoon margarine
1 cup white sugar	

Preheat oven to 350°F. Sift together sifted flour, salt, cinnamon, and baking soda in a medium bowl. Set aside.

Place 12 tablespoons butter, peanut butter, and brown and white sugars in the bowl of an electric mixer. Beat on medium speed until smooth and creamy. Add eggs, one at a time, beating well after each addition. Add vanilla and milk and beat until creamy.

Add dry ingredients, 3 heaping tablespoons at a time, beating well and scraping down bowl after each addition. Add raisins and beat to combine. Scrape down bowl and add oats. Beat to combine. Scrape down bowl and add chocolate chips. Beat to combine.

Grease a baking sheet with 1 tablespoon margarine. Place 12 of cookie dough 2 inches apart on sheet. Bake for 15 minutes, until golden brown. Cool on a wire rack.

While cookies are baking, place heaping teaspoonfuls of the remaining dough on a baking sheet, 1 inch apart. Place baking sheet in freezer for 30 minutes. When dough is frozen, transfer to a covered container, separating layers with waxed paper or plastic wrap. Store in freezer. (Bake frozen cookie dough for 18 minutes.)

In a recipe, "1 cup sifted flour" and "1 cup flour, sifted" are two different measurements. For "1 cup sifted flour," sift flour before measuring. For "1 cup flour, sifted," measure flour and then sift. The sifting process adds volume to the flour. So "1 cup flour, sifted," actually yields more sifted flour than "1 cup sifted flour."

Makes: 4½ dozen cookies (18 servings of 3 cookies each) | 27 minutes (plus 6 minutes to place freezer dough on trays when others are baking and 5 minutes to transfer dough to covered container in freezer) | 15 minutes (18 minutes if starting with frozen cookie dough)

Fudge Nutty Brownies

The combination of peanut butter and chocolate has long been a source of comfort. Add the richness of cashews to the mix and you have nirvana. The beauty of this recipe is that when the warm frosting is poured over the hot baked brownies, the frosting bubbles and percolates into the brownies, so the final cooled dessert actually resembles fudge.

1 (21-ounce) family-size package chewy
    fudge brownie mix
⅔ cup canola oil
¼ cup water
2 eggs
½ cup chopped cashews
1 (12-ounce) package white chocolate
    morsels

4 tablespoons (½ stick) butter
¼ cup creamy peanut butter
½ cup sugar
¼ cup milk
1 teaspoon vanilla

Preheat oven to 350°F. Grease a 13x9-inch baking dish. Place brownie mix, oil, and water in the large bowl of an electric mixer. Beat until blended, about 30 seconds. Add eggs, one at a time, beating each into batter. Add cashews and chocolate morsels, beating just until mixed into batter. Spread batter into prepared baking dish. Bake for 28 minutes, until a wooden skewer inserted in the center comes out clean.

While brownies are baking, melt butter in a small saucepan over medium heat. Add peanut butter, sugar, milk, and vanilla, and stir to combine. Stir constantly, until mixture comes to a boil and sugar is dissolved. Turn heat down to low and cook, stirring constantly for 1 minute. Remove from heat.

Remove baked brownies from oven and place baking dish on a wire rack. Pour warm frosting over hot brownies. Allow frosted brownies to cool at room temperature for 1 hour, until frosting has hardened, then cut them into 2-inch squares. Or, to serve as a warm dessert, allow brownies to cool just until frosting has congealed enough that it is not runny, about 15 minutes. Cut frosted brownies into 4-inch squares and serve topped with a scoop of vanilla ice cream.

Substitute chopped peanuts for cashews, dark chocolate chips for white morsels, or chunky peanut butter for smooth, if you like. Once completely cooled, you can freeze these brownies for up to a month.

Serves: 12 (2 2-inch-square brownies per serving) | Brownies: 10 minutes; Frosting: 6 minutes | 28 minutes | Cooling time: 15 minutes to 1 hour

Grand Marnier Strawberry-Almond Shortcake

Strawberry shortcake is required eating during the succulent berry's season, but with the decadent addition of orange liqueur in this recipe, you can substitute frozen berries all year long and the dessert will be almost as tasty.

2 quarts strawberries, hulled and sliced

⅓ cup Grand Marnier

1 cup sugar, divided

1½ cups flour

2¼ teaspoons baking powder

½ teaspoon baking soda

¼ teaspoon salt

6 tablespoons chilled unsalted butter, cut into ½-inch dice

¾ cup sliced almonds

1½ cups heavy cream, divided

1½ teaspoons almond extract, divided

1½ tablespoons confectioners' sugar

Combine strawberries, liqueur, and ⅔ cup sugar together in a medium bowl. Stir to mix well. Cover and refrigerate until needed.

Preheat oven to 450°F. Place flour, ⅓ cup sugar, baking powder, baking soda, and salt in the bowl of a food processor. Pulse, lightly, to mix. Add butter and pulse until it is cut into flour mixture. Add almonds and pulse until nuts are finely chopped. Transfer flour mixture to a large bowl. Place ¾ cup heavy cream in a measuring cup. Stir in ¾ teaspoon almond extract. Pour cream into dry ingredients and stir with a fork until dough is moist and fluffy.

Place a sheet of parchment paper on a large baking sheet. Divide dough into 8 portions. Using clean hands, form each portion into a flattened patty about 3 inches in diameter and 1½ inches thick. Place on parchment paper about 2 inches apart. Bake until golden, about 13 minutes. Transfer to a wire rack to cool.

While biscuits are baking, place heavy cream in the bowl of an electric mixer and beat until frothy. Slowly add powdered sugar and ¾ teaspoon almond extract, beating constantly until stiff peaks form. Transfer whipped cream to a covered container and refrigerate until needed.

To serve: Crumble each biscuit onto a dessert plate. Top with strawberries and macerated juices. Place a dollop of whipped cream atop each shortcake.

 You can make biscuits up to 2 days ahead. Wrap each individually in aluminum foil until needed. Reheat in a 350°F oven for 5–10 minutes.

For a quick, easy, light dessert, skip the biscuits and serve drunken strawberries instead. Divide macerated strawberries among 4 tulip-shaped wine glasses. Top with a generous dollop of whipped cream. Sprinkle with dry-toasted almonds.

Serves: 8 | 25 minutes | 🕐 13 minutes

Death by Chocolate Mousse Trifle

This dessert requires a little plan-ahead time to put together, but the rewards for your efforts are tenfold. Not only is the presentation elegantly beautiful, the dessert itself is lip-smacking good. And the bonus is that you can spoon leftover trifle into a fresh serving bowl, swirl the top with a spoon, cover, and freeze it for another time. Simply defrost it in the refrigerator and serve. It's even better the second time around.

1 (17-ounce) package frozen Duncan Hines Oven Ready Homestyle Brownies
⅓ cup Bailey's Irish Crème
6 large Heath Bars
1 (3.1-ounce) package Dr. Oetker Mousse Supreme (Dark Chocolate Truffle flavor)
1 (8-ounce) container Cool Whip, thawed

One to 2 days ahead: Preheat oven to 350°F. Bake brownies for 25 minutes, until cooked through but not hardened. Pour Bailey's over hot brownies. Allow to cool. Cover with foil and keep at room temperature for at least 1 day, until ready to assemble trifle.

Early in the day or before dinner: To assemble trifle, break up Heath bars and place in the bowl of a food processor. Pulse until Heath bars are evenly crushed.

Place 1 cup water in the bowl of an electric mixer. Add mousse mix and beat on slow speed until slightly thickened, about 30 seconds. Increase speed to high and beat for 3–5 minutes, until fluffy.

Break up brownies into bite-size pieces and place in a shallow glass bowl, lining bottom and sides. Sprinkle half the crushed Heath bars over the brownies. Spread mousse over brownies. Top with a layer of Cool Whip. Sprinkle remaining crushed Heath bars over trifle. Refrigerate until needed.

 Brownies need to be prepared at least 1 day ahead of time, so that the flavor of the Bailey's marries with the chocolate.

If you prefer, you can bake a packaged brownie mix instead of the freezer-ready brownies. It will add a few minutes time, but you'll only have to use half the brownies for this dessert. If you don't have Bailey's, substitute Kahlùa instead. Dr. Oetker brand mousse is superior, but if you can't find it, substitute Jell O No Bake Chocolate Mousse.

To make individual trifles: Layer trifle, as listed above, into long-stemmed bubble wine glasses or stemless red wine glasses.

Serves: 12 | 20 minutes | 25 minutes

Peach Cobbler

The topping on this quintessential southern classic reminds me of my grandmother's sugar cookies — melt-in-your-mouth delicious. And you'll swear the peaches fell fresh off the tree. You can easily assemble the cobbler early in the day and just pop it in the oven as you sit down to dinner. When you're ready for dessert, you'll be treated to sweet, warm cobbler that just begs for a scoop of vanilla ice cream.

2 cups sugar, divided

1 cup plus 2 tablespoons flour, divided

1 (1-pound) package frozen sliced peaches (about 4 cups)

6 tablespoons cold unsalted butter, cut into ½-inch pieces, plus ½ tablespoon butter

1 teaspoon baking powder

1 teaspoon salt

1 egg, beaten

Early in the day: Stir I cup sugar and 2 tablespoons flour together in a medium bowl. Add frozen peach slices and toss to combine. Butter a I0-inch deep-dish pie plate with ½ tablespoon butter. Pour peach mixture into pie plate and set aside.

Place remaining I cup sugar, I cup flour, baking powder, and salt in a medium bowl. Stir to mix. Add remaining 6 tablespoons butter to the sugar mixture. With clean fingers, combine butter with sugar mixture, until mixture looks like a bowl of small crumbs. Add egg and mix with butter-sugar crumbs using your fingers, until egg is evenly absorbed. (Mixture will be dry.)

Using two forks, spread topping evenly over peach mixture. Cover with plastic wrap and refrigerate until needed.

To bake: Preheat oven to 375°F. Bake cobbler, uncovered, for 40 minutes, or until crust is golden and bubbly. Remove from oven and allow cobbler to rest for 5 minutes before serving.

 Assembling this cobbler earlier in the day is not only time-saving at the dinner hour, but the refrigeration time allows the peaches to thaw. You can bake this cobbler directly after assembling if you prefer. Increase baking time by 5 minutes to compensate for the frozen peaches.

Serves: 4–6 | 17 minutes | 🕐 40 minutes (+ 5 minutes cooling time)

Apple Tart

Autumn spells apple season and nothing warms the heart ... and tummy ... like a warm apple tart, straight from the oven. The beauty of this recipe is that it makes even a novice baker look like a professional pastry chef. You can assemble the tart in about 20 minutes, hours ahead of time. Pop the tart in the oven as you serve dinner and the dessert will be ready when you are.

1 sheet frozen puff pastry (½ of a
    17.3-ounce package), thawed
2 tablespoons butter, divided
¼ cup plus 1 tablespoon apricot preserves
2 sweet-tart apples, like Honeycrisp, Gala,
    or Fuji

1 wedge fresh lemon
3 tablespoons sugar
¼ teaspoon ground cinnamon
¼ teaspoon ground ginger

Early in the day: Unfold puff pastry on a baking sheet that has been lined with parchment paper. Using a fork, prick a 1-inch border around pastry, then prick randomly across the rest of the pastry.

Place 1 tablespoon butter and 1 tablespoon apricot preserves in a small bowl. Microwave for 45 seconds, until butter is melted. Stir to mix. Brush mixture across the entire puff pastry sheet.

Working with 1 apple at a time, cut apple into quarters. Rub cut sides with lemon. Core, peel, and slice apple thinly. Place apple slices, overlapping slightly, into rows atop the pastry. Leave a 1-inch border of pastry around apples. Repeat with remaining apple. Fill in any gaps with any remaining apple slices.

Melt remaining butter in a small bowl in the microwave, about 20 seconds. Brush butter onto apple slices. Mix sugar, cinnamon, and ginger together in a small bowl. Sprinkle mixture over apple slices. Using a paring knife, lightly score pastry at edges of apples on all 4 sides. Fold up the pastry edges and pinch the pastry together at the corners. Cover with aluminum foil and refrigerate until needed.

To bake: Preheat oven to 400°F. Bake tart for 15 minutes. Place ¼ cup apricot preserves in a small bowl and microwave for 45 seconds, until melted. Spoon preserves over apples. Return tart to oven and bake for 10 minutes more. Serve with vanilla ice cream.

For individual tarts, cut pastry into 4 equal squares and press into individual 6-inch (8-ounce) custard cups or ramekins or cups of a maxi-muffin pan. Follow recipe above, dividing apples equally among the 4 tarts.

Serves: 4–6 | 20 minutes | 25 minutes

Pumpkin Satin Pie

Pumpkin pie evokes memories of Thanksgiving turkey and family gatherings. This recipe makes two pies. If you're not cooking for a gang, serve one now and keep one frozen for use another time.

1 (8-ounce) package cream cheese, softened

2 tablespoons plus 1 cup milk

2 tablespoons sugar

1 (8-ounce) container Cool Whip at refrigerator temperature

1 (15-ounce) can pumpkin pie filling

2 (3.4-ounce) packages French vanilla instant pudding mix

1 teaspoon ground cinnamon

½ teaspoon ground ginger

¼ teaspoon ground cloves

2 (6-ounce) prepared graham cracker pie crusts

Place cream cheese, 2 tablespoons milk, and sugar in the bowl of an electric mixer. Beat until creamy. Change beater to the whisk attachment and whisk Cool Whip into cream cheese mixture. Transfer mixture to another bowl. Wash and dry mixer bowl and replace regular beater to electric mixer. Place pumpkin, 1 cup milk, pudding mix, cinnamon, ginger, and cloves in the mixer bowl and beat until creamy. Add Cool Whip mixture and combine on low speed until ingredients are well mixed. Divide the pumpkin mixture equally between the 2 pie crusts. Cover with the inverted plastic lids from prepared pie crusts and freeze for 1 hour or until needed.

 Thaw whole pie in refrigerator for 15 minutes before serving. Or, heat a sharp knife under hot water before cutting slices from frozen pie; thaw them on serving plates at room temperature.

Serves: 12 (each pie serves 6) | 20 minutes | 1 hour

Key Lime Pie

The ultimate comfort dessert in the Florida Keys, real Key lime pie is always yellow — never green — because ripe Key limes are yellow. Don't be tempted to buy the fresh green Key limes offered in the supermarket. They are unripe and don't have any juice in them. Buy bottled juice instead.

¼ cup sliced almonds

3 large eggs, yolks and whites divided

1 (14-ounce) can Eagle Brand Sweetened Condensed Milk

½ cup bottled Key lime juice

1 (6-ounce) Shortbread Ready Crust

¼ teaspoon cream of tartar

½ cup sugar

Preheat oven to 375°F. Place almonds in a small nonstick skillet over low heat. Toast almonds, stirring frequently, for 2–3 minutes. When almonds start to brown, remove from heat and set aside to cool.

Place egg yolks in the bowl of an electric mixer and beat until frothy. Add sweetened condensed milk and beat to combine. Slowly pour in Key lime juice and beat until mixture is creamy, about 1 minute.

Sprinkle almonds on the bottom of the pie crust. Pour filling into crust and set aside.

Wash and dry mixer bowl and beaters thoroughly. Place egg whites in bowl and beat with electric mixer until medium peaks form. Add cream of tartar and beat to combine. Slowly add sugar, beating constantly, until stiff peaks form.

Spread meringue over pie, making sure it seals the crust. Bake for 15 minutes, until meringue is golden. Cool at room temperature for 5 minutes. Refrigerate until chilled. (If you don't want to bother making the meringue, bake pie for 10 minutes, chill, and top with a dollop of Cool Whip.)

 Nellie & Joe's brand bottled Key lime juice is available in many supermarkets. Go to their Web site (www.keylimejuice.com) to find a list of online retailers and supermarkets carrying their product. The bottled juice does have a shelf life. Freeze it in ½-cup portions.

Serves: 6–8 | 15 minutes | 15 minutes

Southern Banana Pudding

As the old James Taylor song goes: "In my mind, I'm goin' to Carolina" with every bite of this creamy, old-fashioned, classic Southern comfort.

4 cups milk

2 (3-ounce) boxes Jell-O Cook & Serve Vanilla Pudding

2 teaspoons banana extract or banana liqueur

1 (12-ounce) box Nilla Wafers or other vanilla wafers

6 ripe bananas, thinly sliced

1 (8-ounce) carton Cool Whip, thawed at refrigerator temperature

Place milk and pudding in a large saucepan over medium heat. Cook pudding, stirring frequently, until it begins to thicken. Continue cooking, stirring constantly, until pudding just comes to a boil. Remove from heat immediately.

While pudding is cooking, place a layer of vanilla wafers on the bottom of a 7x11-inch baking dish. Cover wafers with half the banana slices. Pour half the pudding over the wafers and bananas. Repeat layers, ending with pudding. Top with Cool Whip. Refrigerate until needed.

 For a fancier presentation, eliminate the Cool Whip and try this easy baked meringue instead: Just before serving, preheat oven to 350°F. Beat 4 egg whites in a medium bowl until frothy. Add ½ teaspoon cream of tartar and beat until stiff peaks form. Add 6 tablespoons sugar, 1 tablespoon at a time, beating until stiff. Beat in 1 teaspoon almond extract. Spread meringue over pudding and bake until golden on top, about 15 minutes.

Serves: 10–12 | 18 minutes

Blackberry Cheesecake Bites

Everyone loves a bite of cheesecake and this recipe delivers bite, after bite, after bite. These bite-size, cheesecakes freeze well, so make a double batch and any time you need a quick dessert, or maybe just a personal comfort food fix, head for the freezer. They defrost in minutes.

1 (8-ounce) package cream cheese, softened at room temperature

1 large egg

¾ cup sugar

1 teaspoon vanilla

24 Mini Nilla Wafers

1 cup blackberry pie filling

Preheat oven to 350°F. Place cream cheese, egg, sugar, and vanilla in the large bowl of an electric mixer. Beat until creamy, about 3 minutes.

Line a 24-count miniature muffin pan with paper miniature cupcake liners. Place 1 miniature vanilla wafer in the bottom of each paper, flat side down. Fill each cup three-quarters full with cheesecake mixture. Bake for 18 minutes, until cheesecake is set. Allow to cool 5 minutes. Place in a shallow covered container and refrigerate or freeze until needed. (Makes 24 miniature cheesecake bites.)

To serve: Up to several hours ahead, place a teaspoonful of blackberry pie filling atop each mini cheesecake. Transfer cheesecakes to a serving platter and refrigerate until needed. (Thaw frozen cheesecakes before topping them with pie filling.)

You can make these cheesecakes in a regular-size cupcake pan. Place 3 miniature vanilla wafers in the bottom of each cupcake liner. Fill three-quarters full with cheesecake mixture and bake for 20 minutes. Makes 8 cream cheese cupcakes. You can use any of your favorite pie filling flavors for topping the cheesecakes or top with Hot Fudge Sauce (page 112). The fudge sauce hardens when it is refrigerated.

Serves: 8 (3 cheesecake bites per serving) | 17 minutes | 18 minutes

Cherry-Fudge Babycakes |

From pantry to freezer, these decadently chocolate babycakes take under an hour to prepare. And because you can make them at your leisure and freeze them until you need a quick chocolate fix or a no-fuss company dessert, you can almost call them "fast food."

1 (18.25-ounce) package chocolate fudge cake mix

1 (21-ounce) can cherry pie filling

3 eggs

1 teaspoon almond extract

5 tablespoons butter

1 cup sugar

⅓ cup milk

1 cup semisweet chocolate chips

Preheat oven to 350°F. Place paper liners in muffin cups. Place cake mix, pie filling, eggs, and almond extract in the bowl of an electric mixer. Beat until well blended, about 2 minutes. Spoon batter into paper liners, filling them a little more than half full. Bake for 17 minutes or until an inserted wooden skewer comes out clean.

While cakes are baking, prepare frosting. Melt butter in a small saucepan over medium heat. Add sugar and milk. Bring to a boil, stirring constantly, for 1 minute. Remove frosting from heat. Stir in chocolate chips until melted and smooth.

Remove cakes from oven. Pulling gently on the paper liners, remove cakes from pan and cool on a wire rack for 2 minutes. Remove paper liners from cakes and transfer them to a parchment or waxed paper–lined baking sheet.

Using a spoon, drizzle frosting onto cakes, completely covering tops and allowing frosting to run down the sides and pool on the paper. Using a table knife, spread the pooled frosting up the sides of the cakes. (If frosting gets too hard to run down sides of cakes, reheat for a few seconds.)

Using a firm spatula, transfer frosted cakes to 2 parchment or waxed paper–lined large covered containers. Freeze babycakes until needed.

To serve: Defrost each cake on an individual dessert plate for about 20 minutes. Serve with a scoop of ice cream on the side.

 You'll need two, 6-count (6-inch, 8-ounce) maxi-muffin pans and paper liners for this recipe. You can also bake this recipe as a sheet cake. Place batter in a 13x9-inch greased baking pan and bake for 40 minutes or until an inserted wooden skewer comes out clean.

Serves: 12 (1 babycake per serving) | 13 minutes; frosting cakes: 14 minutes | ⓥ 19 minutes (including cool time)

Orange Rum Cake

This Orange Rum Cake freezes beautifully. Make cake ahead and freeze it until you need it, or divide it into quarters and freeze portions for a quick, last-minute dessert. Each quarter serves four people and defrosts in 15 minutes.

1 tablespoon butter, margarine, or Crisco
¼ cup sugar
1 (3.4-ounce) package lemon instant pudding
1 (18-ounce) package orange cake mix
4 eggs
½ cup water

½ cup canola oil
¾ cup orange juice concentrate, divided
¼ cup dark rum
2 cups confectioners' sugar
Orange slices (optional)

Preheat oven to 350°F. Grease and sugar a bundt pan. Place pudding, cake mix, eggs, water, canola oil, and ½ cup orange juice concentrate in the bowl of an electric mixer. Beat for 2 minutes, until smooth and creamy. Transfer batter to the bundt pan and bake for 35–40 minutes, until an inserted wooden skewer comes out clean.

While cake is baking, make glaze. Place ¼ cup orange juice concentrate, rum, and confectioners' sugar in a medium bowl. Whisk until smooth. Set aside until needed.

Remove baked cake from oven and unmold it onto a large platter. Using a wooden skewer, poke holes all over the top of the cake. Spoon glaze over warm cake, allowing glaze to run down sides of cake and pool onto the platter. Scoop the glaze off the platter and spoon it over the cake repeatedly, making sure inner and outer sides of the cake are covered. (You'll have a small pool of glaze surrounding the cake. Serve a section of it with each slice of cake.) Garnish with orange slices, if desired.

For lemon or lime cake, substitute fresh juice or frozen lemonade or limeade concentrate for the orange juice concentrate. You can eliminate the rum if desired.

Serves: 12–15 | 22 minutes | 35–40 minutes

Butter-Pecan Bundt Cake

Cakes don't get any easier to make than this one. Flavorful and moist, it also can be successfully frozen. When unexpected guests drop in or when you need to serve dessert in a hurry, the answer is as close as your freezer.

1 (18-ounce) package Betty Crocker Butter Pecan Cake mix
⅔ cup canola oil
1 cup water
1 cup chopped pecans, divided
1 (14.5-ounce) can pecan-coconut cake frosting

Preheat oven to 350°F. Coat a bundt pan with vegetable cooking spray. Place cake mix, oil, water, ½ cup pecans, and frosting in the large bowl of an electric mixer. Beat for 2 minutes, until mixture is well blended. Sprinkle remaining ½ cup pecans in the bottom of the bundt pan. Pour batter into pan. Bake for 45 minutes, or until an inserted wooden skewer comes out clean.

Cool thoroughly in pan (2 hours) before unmolding on a serving platter. Serve with butter-pecan ice cream or a dollop of whipped cream.

 Cut uneaten cake in portions that will serve 4 people. Wrap in a double layer of plastic wrap, then in aluminum foil. Place in a zipper bag. When you need a quick dessert, take a portion from the freezer and remove foil and plastic wrap. Defrost at room temperature, then lightly cover with plastic wrap until serving.

Serves: 12 | 5–10 minutes | 🕐 45 minutes (+ 2 hours cooling time)

A well-stocked larder is a cook's best friend. Keep these staples and supplies on hand and you can prepare any recipe in this cookbook at a moment's notice.

Pantry

PRODUCE

bananas

garlic

onions: sweet like Vidalia, red

potatoes: russet, sweet

shallots

squash: butternut, spaghetti

tomatoes: slicing, grape, plum or Roma, green

BAKING SUPPLIES

baking powder

baking soda

Bisquick

buttermilk (powdered)

cake and biscuit mixes: Betty Crocker Butter Pecan Cake mix, chocolate fudge cake, orange cake, Chewy Fudge Brownie Mix, Jiffy Buttermilk Biscuit Mix

cake frosting: pecan-coconut frosting

chocolate: unsweetened chocolate squares, semisweet chocolate chips, white chocolate morsels, Heath bars

cornstarch

Crisco

Eagle Brand Sweetened Condensed Milk

evaporated milk

extracts: vanilla, almond, banana

flour (all-purpose)

Nilla Wafers (regular and mini)

oats: Quaker Old-Fashioned, Quaker Quick Cooking

pie crusts (Ready): graham cracker, shortbread

pie fillings: pumpkin, blackberry, cherry

pudding mixes: Dr. Oetker Mousse Supreme (Dark Chocolate Truffle flavor), French vanilla instant pudding, Jell-O Cook & Serve Vanilla Pudding, lemon instant pudding

sugar: granulated white, confectioners', light brown, dark brown

syrup: light corn, maple

SEASONINGS AND MIXES

bread crumbs (dried): panko, Italian seasoned, seasoned fish breading mix

broth and stock: beef, chicken, College Inn White Wine & Herb Culinary Broth, College Inn Rotisserie Chicken Bold Stock, College Inn Culinary Thai Coconut Curry Broth, College Inn Beef Sirloin Bold Stock

croutons

dried fruits: cherries, cranberries, dates, apricots, raisins, currants

jams/jellies/marmalades: orange marmalade, red currant jelly, apricot preserves, blackberry preserves

nuts: glazed pecans, peanuts, cashews

pepper: cracked pepper, peppercorns, ground pepper, white pepper, crushed red pepper flakes

potatoes: Four Cheese Mashed, Loaded Baked Mashed (Idahoan)

ramen chicken-flavored noodles

salt: kosher or coarse, table

sauce mixes: Creamy Garlic Alfredo Sauce, Hollandaise Sauce (McCormick)

soup: "Darn Good" Chili Mix (Bear Creek), Chicken Noodle Soup Mix (Bear Creek)

spices: allspice, basil, cayenne pepper, celery seed, chili powder, cinnamon, cloves, cream of tartar, cumin, curry powder (mild Sharwood's or Madras), dried onion flakes, dry mustard, garlic powder, ground ginger, marjoram, McCormick Garlic Herb Seasoning Blend, nutmeg, oregano, parsley, poppy seeds, sesame seeds, tarragon, thyme, turmeric, wasabi powder

taco seasoning mix

MISCELLANEOUS
flour tortillas (burrito-size)

juices: apple, Key lime

liquor: beer, white wine, sherry, Crème de Cassis, Grand Marnier, Bailey's Irish Crème, dark rum, Triple Sec, Jim Beam bourbon whiskey

pasta: dried cheese tortellini, ditalini or tube-shaped, miniature penne or elbow macaroni, no-cook flat lasagna noodles, linguine, spaghetti, angel hair or thin spaghetti, tagliatelle or fettuccine, egg noodles, orzo

peanut butter: smooth, chunky

pizza crusts (Mama Mary's Gourmet Pizza Thin & Crispy Crust)

rice: basmati, jasmine, arborio

taco shells

tortilla chips (restaurant-style white)

CANNED GOODS
anchovies

artichoke hearts

beans: black, butter, Great Northern, red kidney, baby lima

cheddar cheese soup

chick peas

clams (chopped)

corn (cream-style)

enchilada sauce

olives (black sliced)

pork and beans

refried beans

salmon (wild Alaskan red)

shrimp (small)

tomato paste

tomato sauce

tomatoes: crushed or puree; Diced with Basil, Garlic, and Oregano; Hunt's Fire Roasted Diced; Petite Cut Diced with Garlic and Olive Oil; Petite Cut Diced

tuna (white in water)

JAR OR BOTTLED GOODS

artichoke tapenade

Asian sweet chili sauce

banana pepper rings (mild)

barbecue sauce (smoky flavor)

basil pesto

capers

clam juice

cranberry relish

fish sauce

hoisin sauce

honey

horseradish sauce

hot sauce or Tabasco sauce

ketchup

mayonnaise

molasses

mustard: honey, Dijon, raspberry honey, other fruit-flavored honey

oils: light olive, extra-virgin olive, canola, olive oil spray, toasted sesame

olives: kalamata black oil-cured, pimento-stuffed green

onions (small whole cooked)

pasta sauce: sweet basil, marinara

pickles: sweet gherkins

roasted red peppers

salad dressing Zesty Italian

salsa

soy sauce

vinegars: white, red wine, rice, cider, balsamic

whole baby clams

worcestershire sauce

Freezer

BREADS

English muffins

breads: whole-grain, white, sourdough, cinnamon-raisin, Italian, ciabatta, artisan, pita

buns and rolls: hamburger, brat, 3-inch rolls or Walmart White Dollar Rolls, hoagie

STAPLE INGREDIENTS

bell peppers (red, yellow, and orange): Keep a bag of frozen bell peppers on hand for cooked dishes.

bread crumbs (fresh): (See how-to instructions in Time- and Money-saving Tips section)

butter: Defrost as needed and store in the refrigerator.

cheese (shredded, crumbled): blue, Swiss, Monterey Jack, sharp cheddar, mild cheddar, 4-Cheese Mexican, Pizza! Shredded Mozzarella & Cheddar, Sargento Authentic Mexican Artisan Blend, 6 Cheese Italian, Colby and Monterey Jack

citrus zest: Grate orange and lemon peel and store in zipper bag. (See how-to instructions in Time- and Money-saving Tips section)

fruits: raspberries, mixed berries, sliced peaches

herbs: Snip fresh flat-leaf parsley, dill, basil, rosemary, and tarragon and store in a zipper bag. (See how-to instructions in

Time- and Money-saving Tips section)

juice concentrates: apple, orange

Ling Ling Potstickers Vegetable Dumplings

mushrooms (sliced): *(See how-to instructions in Time- and Money-saving Tips)*

nuts: Keep nuts frozen so that they don't turn rancid. Keep on hand: walnuts, sliced almonds, slivered almonds, sunflower seeds, pine nuts

potatoes: Country-Style Hash Brown; crinkle-cut French fried

vegetables: spinach, Asian vegetables, peas, corn

MEAT, SEAFOOD, AND POULTRY

bacon (Canadian, smoked): Separate slices and roll each up in cling wrap so that the wrap is between each slice. Store in a freezer-weight zipper bag. Peel off as many frozen slices as you need

beef (lean ground)

bratwurst (Original Flavor Johnsonville)

chicken breasts (boneless, skinless)

Cornish hens

flounder fillets

ham: Dice leftover ham and package in ½-cup portions in two layers of plastic wrap. Store in a freezer-weight zipper bag.

pork loin (boneless)

pork sausage (Jimmy Dean's Maple Pork Sausage and Spicy Pork Sausage): Wrap 4-ounce portions in plastic wrap and store in freezer-weight zipper bags.

pork tenderloins

roast (rump, round, or chuck)

shrimp (uncooked, shell on)

steak (top sirloin): Cut 1½ inches thick

turkey (ground)

DESSERT STAPLES

Cool Whip

Duncan Hines Oven Ready Homestyle Brownies

pastry: puff pastry sheets, puff pastry shells

Rhodes or other frozen dough rolls

Refrigerator

PRODUCE

apples: Fuji, Gala, Honeycrisp

asparagus

bell peppers (fresh): red, orange, yellow, green

cabbage (3-color slaw mix)

carrots: baby, shredded

celery

chile peppers: jalapeño, poblano

grapes

green beans

herbs (fresh): mint

juices: orange, lemon

leafy greens: baby spinach, iceberg lettuce, romaine lettuce hearts

mushrooms (fresh): portobello, white button, brown button, shiitake

oranges

scallions

strawberries

sugar snap peas

sweet corn

Yukon Gold potatoes: These potatoes have a higher sugar content than russet potatoes. Store them in a paper bag or perforated plastic bag in crisper drawer.

DAIRY

Boursin garlic and herb cheese spread

butter: salted, unsalted

cheese (chunk): mozzarella; Kraft White Sharp Cheddar, Swiss & Parmesan; pepper jack, tomato-basil feta cheese, Brie, baby swiss

cheese (sliced): Swiss, Muenster, mozzarella

cottage cheese

cream cheese: whipped, block

EggBeaters: Southwestern-style, with yolk

eggs (large)

half-and-half

heavy cream

margarine

milk

Parmesan cheese: grated, shredded

plain yogurt

sour cream

sour cream ranch dip (like T. Marzetti)

MEAT, SEAFOOD, AND POULTRY

cold cuts: sliced ham, sliced salami, sliced pepperoni, smoked turkey

fish fillets: salmon, tilapia

ham steak

imitation crabmeat

rotisserie chicken (supermarket delicatessen)

MISCELLANEOUS

guacamole

herb pastes: Gourmet Garden finely ground herb pastes last for months and eliminate mincing, chopping, and snipping prep time. You'll find them in the refrigerated produce section of your supermarket. Be sure you have ginger-root and garlic. Other pastes are red chili pepper, cilantro, basil, and lemongrass.

Marie's Creamy Italian Garlic Dressing

Pillsbury Golden Layers Honey Butter Biscuits

Equipment and Supplies

- **Cooking oil pump sprayer:** Misto is a popular brand found at most stores that sell kitchen supplies. Light olive oil or canola oil works best in the sprayer. Using the sprayer is more economical; allows for a more even, controllable spray; and is free of the chemicals commonly found in commercial aerosol cooking sprays.

- **Two sets of measuring cups:** You should have one set of measuring cups for liquids — 1-cup, 2-cup, and/or 4-cup glass or plastic calibrated in ounces — and one set for measuring dry ingredients — 1 cup, ½ cup, ⅓ cup, ¼ cup. Dry ingredients need to be leveled off with a knife.

- **Parchment paper:** You can substitute butcher paper or waxed paper for parchment paper when flash-freezing items, but don't make such a substitution when baking. You do not have to grease a baking sheet if you line it with parchment paper.

- **Microplane grater:** One of a cook's best investments is an ultra-sharp microplane grater (about $15), available at most stores that sell kitchenware. You can grate lemon, lime, or orange peel in mere seconds. You can finely grate gingerroot, garlic, onion, even chocolate.

- **Maxi, mini, and standard muffin pans:** Maxi-muffin pans have 6 (6-inch) cups, each holding about 8 ounces. Mini-muffin pans have 24 (2-inch) cups, each holding about 1 ounce. You'll need the maxi pan for Cherry-Fudge Babycakes and the mini pan for the Neapolitan Meatballs. Busy Morning Breakfast Cupcakes are made in a standard muffin pan.

- **Round ramekins:** You'll need 4 (¼-cup) round ramekins for Sunflower Eggs Benedict, 6 (1½-cup) ramekins for Chicken Pot Pies and for Cottage Pies, and 4 (½-cup) ramekins for the Almost Twice-Baked Potatoes.

- **Round biscuit cutter:** You'll need a biscuit or cookie cutter ring that is 3 inches in diameter to make the Thai Salmon Cakes and to form the ground beef patties for Burger Mania.

- **Metal skewers:** Meat, chicken, and seafood stays in place better if the skewers have flat shafts instead of round ones. You'll need them for the recipes in Cookout Kabobs.

- **Small appliances:** You can make the sandwiches in Panini, Panini, Panini without a George Foreman Grill or Panini Press, but they both save time and are easy to operate. You'll need a slow cooker or Crockpot for the Slow Cooker recipes in this book. You should have a waffle iron to make Bacon–Four Cheese Waffles. Many of the recipes call for a blender, food processor, electric mixer, or microwave oven.

- **Other pans you'll need:** Broiler pan, nonstick skillets and saucepans (small, medium, large), pizza pan, wok or stir-fry pan, baking sheets, deep-dish and regular pie plates, bundt pan, baking pans (7x11-inch, 9x13-inch, 8x8-inch).

- Assemble all ingredients and equipment prior to starting a recipe. This will take a couple of minutes, but it saves valuable time and steps while actually cooking.

- Buy several bundles of fresh herbs when they are inexpensive and plentiful in the summer season. When you have an extra hour or so to yourself some Saturday, put a movie on your DVD player. Get a pair of kitchen scissors, a bowl, and some zipper bags. Snip your herbs into the bowl as you watch the movie. Transfer each type of herb to a zipper bag, label, and freeze. One snipped bunch will last you for months. Basil, dill, parsley, cilantro, and chives are good herbs to have in your freezer pantry. The frozen herbs will keep in the freezer for a year, guaranteeing you can always cook with fresh herbs.

- Buy red, yellow, and orange bell peppers when they are in season and not so expensive. Chop or cut them into slices. Freeze peppers on a baking sheet, then store in a zipper bag in the freezer until needed. They are a great substitute for fresh.

- Buy several pounds of butter when you find it on sale and freeze it until needed. Butter freezes very well. Should you buy salted or unsalted butter? Salt is used as a preservative that is not needed as long as you store the butter in the refrigerator. If you do use salted butter, reduce the salt in a recipe by ¼ teaspoon per ½ cup of butter used. Always use unsalted butter when baking.

- Freeze leftover chicken, vegetable, or beef broth as well as extra fresh orange, lemon, and lime juice or canned coconut milk in ice cube trays. Place cubes in labeled zipper bags and freeze until needed. Thaw cubes overnight in refrigerator or microwave at 30-second intervals until defrosted. Lots of recipes call for just small amounts of these ingredients and you'll have them readily on hand.

- When you find lemons on sale, buy a bag. (Supermarkets often sell their "ripe" lemons in a large bag at a considerable discount.) Use your microplane grater (see page 132) to grate the peel and then freeze this zest, wrapped in plastic wrap, until needed. Squeeze the lemons and freeze juice in ½-cup containers or ice cube trays (pop juice cubes into zipper bags). Keep them in the freezer until needed. (You can do this with limes and oranges too.) You'll have fresh juice and grated lemon peel on hand for months. To get more juice from a lemon, heat it in the microwave for 30 seconds, then roll it on the counter under the palm of your hand.

- Buttermilk has a short shelf life, so most cooks don't keep it on hand. Buttermilk can be frozen, however. Freeze buttermilk in 1-cup portions. Thaw in the refrigerator and shake before using. The texture will be slightly different, but it won't affect the outcome of the recipe. Even easier and more economical, you can purchase dried buttermilk in your supermarket's baking section and prepare the amount you need by simply adding water to the mix.

- Don't throw away your stale bread. Pulse it in a food processor to make fresh bread crumbs. Place crumbs in a zipper bag and freeze until needed. The bread crumbs will keep up to a year.

- Buy fresh mushrooms in bulk at your local price club, which will make the price per pound much cheaper. Remove the stems and wipe them clean with wet paper toweling. Cut the mushrooms with an egg slicer. Place them in a single layer on parchment paper or waxed paper on a baking sheet. Freeze for 30 minutes. Transfer sliced mushrooms to freezer bags for storage and freeze for up to 3 months. You'll spend a little time upfront prepping the mushrooms, but when it comes time to cook, they'll be at your fingertips.

- Blue cheese is expensive but a little goes a long, long way. Keep crumbled blue cheese in the freezer (it can stay frozen for months) and just chip off what you need with a fork. The crumbled bits will defrost instantly.

- Recipes often call for only a couple of marshmallows. Kept in the pantry, they will harden and get stale. Keep marshmallows in the freezer instead. They will stay fresh for a long time.

- If you buy meat in quantity, the price per pound is often less. Prepare several different marinades, such as the ones in the Cookout Kabobs recipe in this book. Place desired amount of meat and marinade in a large zipper bag, label, and freeze them. Then simply take one package out of the freezer the night before you need it and place it in refrigerator to defrost during the day. You'll be ready to grill at night.

- To easily get tomato paste out of the can, open both ends. Remove one lid. Push on other lid with handle of a wooden spoon to get paste out of can. If you only need a tablespoon or two, place the remainder on a piece of cling wrap, form into a cigar-shaped roll and freeze. When a recipe calls for a tablespoon or two of tomato paste, simply cut off what you need.

- Microwave garlic cloves for 10–15 seconds and the peels will slide right off. Whole cloves impart the mildest garlic flavor to foods, followed in intensity by sliced, chopped, and minced. Smashed cloves are the most garlicky.

- To easily peel peaches or tomatoes, cut an "x" into the bottom of each piece of fruit. Drop fruit into boiling water for 10 seconds. Remove with a slotted spoon and run under cool water. The skin will peel right off.

- To chop an onion fast: Peel onion and cut it in half lengthwise through the root end. Make uniform cuts from stem to root end, leaving root end intact. Turn onion ninety degrees and make uniform cuts across the onion, working toward the root end. Discard the root end. You'll have chopped onions in minutes.

- Don't buy onions that have soft spots, a strong smell, or green sprouts. Don't store them in plastic bags or in the refrigerator. Keep them in a cool, dark place away from potatoes, which cause onions to spoil more quickly.

- Many recipes call for a sprinkling of flour or sugar, which is difficult to do evenly with a spoon. Buy inexpensive shakers for flour, sugar, and powdered sugar and you'll better control the coverage.

- Instead of greasing and flouring baking pans, grease and sugar them. You'll eliminate any floury film, and the sides and bottom of the pan will have a sweet coating that won't interfere with the flavor of the baked goods. When doing cut-out cookies, coat your rolling surface with powdered sugar instead of flour.

- To cook bacon for a large group, use the oven. Preheat oven to 350°F. Place bacon strips on a rimmed baking sheet lined with aluminum foil. Bake bacon for 20 minutes or until cooked through and crispy. Drain on paper toweling. To reduce the amount of spattering grease when you are frying bacon on the stove, sprinkle a little flour in the pan before adding the bacon.

- A couple of tricks guarantee perfect hard-boiled eggs every time. Place eggs in a large sauce-pan covered by 1 inch water. Don't crowd them or they may bump into each other. Bring to boil over high heat. Cover pot and immediately remove it from heat. Allow eggs to sit in the hot water for 10 minutes. Drain eggs, then rinse with cool water. Place eggs in a bowl of ice water for a few minutes, which makes them easier to peel. To peel, crack egg all around on a hard surface, then roll the egg between your hands to release the inner membrane. Hold the egg under the water tap and peel, starting at the large end (not the pointy end), where the air pocket will allow you easier entry.

- The keys to successfully beating egg whites are a clean bowl and beaters and room temperature egg whites. Add ⅛ teaspoon cream of tartar per egg white to increase their stability and volume. If a recipe calls for soft peaks, the whites will droop slightly. For stiff peaks, the whites will stand upright when beaters are removed. Overbeaten egg whites will look curdled.

- When you are baking, measure each dry ingredient over a shallow bowl. Put the overflow back in the container to save mess and money.

- The first thing to do when making a pasta dish is to put a large pot of water over high heat and bring it to a boil. Although pasta takes only a short time to cook, it takes much longer for the pot of water to come to a boil. The main secret to successfully making pasta is to use enough water, but here are a few other tips: Add 1½ tablespoons salt (per pound of pasta) to the water and add pasta gradually so that the water maintains a boil. Cook pasta, uncovered, until al dente (firm to the bite), stirring occasionally to prevent pasta from sticking. Follow package instructions for timing, because pastas vary in size and thickness among manufacturers. Drain pasta but do not rinse it. Toss with sauce immediately. (For a pasta salad, drain pasta, rinse with cold water, and drain again.)

Did you know?

- Both semisweet and bittersweet chocolate contain chocolate liquor (essence of the cocoa bean) and sugar. Bittersweet has more chocolate liquor, so it has a stronger, more intense chocolate flavor. You can use the two interchangeably in recipes.

- Dutch process and regular cocoa powder are different. Dutch process is regular cocoa powder that's been treated with an alkaline solution such as baking soda, which mellows the bitter flavor, making it richer and deeper in color. (The process was invented in Holland, hence the name.) Regular cocoa powder is naturally tart and acidic.

- Coconut milk and cream of coconut should not be substituted for each other. Coconut milk is the liquid extracted from pressed coconut meat that has been mixed with water. (The fat will rise to the surface in the can; simply stir it back into the liquid.) Cream of coconut is almost all sugar, used most often in desserts and drinks.

- The color of a bell pepper indicates how ripe it is. A green bell pepper is not ripe and its taste is strong and bitter. As the pepper matures, it changes color — yellow, orange, red — and gets milder. Red bell peppers are the mildest in flavor.

- Flat-leaf parsley, also known as Italian parsley, has fairly large, smooth, uncurled leaves that look like celery leaves. It is usually the parsley called for in recipes. Curly parsley is milder in flavor and is often used as a garnish, but you can use curly or flat interchangeably.

- Pine nuts are edible seeds from several varieties of pine trees. They are generally pricey because they are harvested by hand from pinecones, then the hard casings are removed. You'll find the best price by buying in bulk from your local price club. Pine nuts are high in protein, but they go rancid quickly, so keep them in the freezer.

- The government guideline for freshness dating of spices is four years for whole spices and two years for ground spices. It is believed that after a period of time, flavor components of the spices begin to dissipate. If you are unsure how old your spices are, smell them. If they smell spicy and strong, keep them. If not, replace them. Store spices in a cupboard or drawer, away from all heat sources. Glass or rigid plastic containers are the best for storing spices.

- Sea salt is de rigueur in culinary circles these days, but all table salt originated in the sea. Mined salt is actually salt that settled to the bottom of the sea in ancient times. Instead of buying expensive sea salt, buy kosher salt, which is also a coarse salt but cheaper.

- One cup self-rising flour equals 1 cup all-purpose flour plus ½ teaspoon salt plus 1½ teaspoons baking powder, so if you encounter a recipe requiring self-rising flour, don't buy it; make your own.

- When a recipe calls for chopping food into dice, approximate sizes are: large — ¾ inch; medium — ½ inch; small — ¼ inch; fine (or minced) — ⅛ inch.

- Eggs are sold by weight, and different sizes could make a difference in how a recipe turns out. Extra-large eggs yield 4 tablespoons, large equals 3¼ tablespoons, and medium equals 3 tablespoons. Follow egg size specifications when baking, but for non-baking recipes requiring fewer than 4 eggs, you can make a one-to-one substitution. If your recipe calls for more than 4 eggs, here are your equivalents: for 4 large eggs use 4 extra-large or 5 medium eggs; for 5 large eggs use 4 extra-large or 6 medium eggs; for 6 large eggs use 5 extra-large or 7 medium eggs.

- Remembering measurement equivalents helps when cutting a recipe in half or doubling it. One gallon equals 4 quarts; 1 quart equals 2 pints; 1 pint equals 2 cups; 1 cup equals 16 tablespoons; ½ cup equals 8 tablespoons; ⅓ cup equals 5 tablespoons plus 1 teaspoon; ¼ cup equals 4 tablespoons; 1 tablespoon equals 3 teaspoons.

- Use one-third the amount of dried herbs if substituting them for fresh herbs. For example, use 1 teaspoon dried basil instead of 1 tablespoon snipped fresh basil.